The
Stakeholder
Strategy

The Stakeholder Strategy

Profiting from Collaborative Business Relationships

ANN SVENDSEN

Berrett-Koehler Publishers, Inc.
San Francisco

Berrett-Koehler Publishers, Inc.
450 Sansome Street, Suite 1200
San Francisco, CA 94111-3320
Tel: (415) 288-0260   Fax: (415) 362-2512
http://www.bkpub.com

Ordering Information

Individual sales. Berrett-Koehler publications are available through most bookstores. They can also be ordered direct from Berrett-Koehler at the address above.

Quantity sales. Special discounts are available on quantity purchases by corporations, associations, and others. For details, contact the "Special Sales Department" at the Berrett-Koehler address above.

Orders for college textbook/course adoption use. Please contact Berrett-Koehler Publishers at the address above.

Orders by U.S. trade bookstores and wholesalers. Please contact Publishers Group West, 1700 Fourth St., Berkeley, CA 94710. Tel: (510) 528–1444; Fax: (510) 528-3444.

Printed in the United States of America

Printed on acid-free and recycled paper that is composed of 85% recovered fiber, including 15% postconsumer waste.

Library of Congress Cataloging-in-Publication Data

Svendsen, Ann, 1954–
    The stakeholder strategy : profiting from collaborative business relationships / Ann Svendsen — 1st ed.
        p. cm.
    Includes bibliographical references and index.
    ISBN 1-57675-047-7 (alk. paper)
    1. Business networks. 2. Social responsibility of business. 3. Social accounting.   I. Title.
    HD69.S8S9   1998
    658.8'12dc21   98-35917
                                                    CIP

First Edition
01 00 99 98   10 9 8 7 6 5 4 3 2 1

Copyediting and proofreading: PeopleSpeak
Interior design and production: Joel Friedlander, Marin Bookworks
Indexing: Thérèse Shere
Cover design: Richard Adelson

For Bob, Kai and Del
my guiding lights

Contents

Preface

This book was supposed to be about social auditing—the practice of systematically recording, presenting, and interpreting a company's nonfinancial or "social" accounts. While the book does address how companies measure the impact of their activities on their stakeholders—customers, shareholders, employees, suppliers, communities—it focuses on what I see to be the bigger picture for social auditing—the kinds of relationships that a company develops with its stakeholders. Specifically, the book zeros in on how companies build long-term, mutually beneficial, collaborative stakeholder relationships.

This book actually began in late 1995 when I was asked to prepare a policy framework for a social audit being conducted by Vancouver City Savings Credit Union ("VanCity Credit Union") in Vancouver, Canada. In a study by the Society of Management Accountants of Canada, VanCity Credit Union had been ranked below the "big banks" for disclosure of nonfinancial information. Given that the credit union prided itself on being a leader in the corporate social responsibility (CSR) area, its managers decided to increase the rigor of their measurement and reporting systems. They needed a road map to point the way.

Looking for some practical advice on how a company could measure and improve its nonfinancial or "social" performance, I read books like *Beyond the Bottom Line* by Joel Makower and Alan Reder's *75 Best Business Practices for Socially Responsible Companies*. These books provided a rationale for why companies should be socially responsible and how doing so could help the bottom line as well as create social benefits. But they didn't address my questions about how to conduct a social audit or about how companies could use that information to improve their social performance.

Meanwhile, I noticed that corporate social responsibility was receiving more media attention. The public was stepping up pressure on corporations to pick up the slack in the wake of government cutbacks. The severe job cuts and the exorbitant salaries of senior executives in major North American corporations, driven upward by soaring stock values, reinforced the rising tide of public and media pressure for greater corporate accountability.

CEOs of some of North America's largest corporations were also starting to pay attention—especially given the runaway success of companies like The Body Shop and Ben and Jerry's Ice Cream that have nurtured a reputation for being socially responsible. Increasing consumer interest in ethical investing and the media-led attack on American-based garment manufacturers over the use of child labor in Third World factories also caught the attention of corporate executives and boards of directors. Inside and outside corporate boardrooms, questions were again being raised about the social responsibilities of corporations. What should companies be responsible for? How much is enough? Who decides?

Unfortunately, the academic literature dealing with corporate social responsibility was of little help in answering these questions. Furthermore, social auditing and accounting research did not establish a clear and direct link between corporate social responsibility measures and profitability. The causal link argued in Reder's and Makower's path-breaking books was not substantiated when placed under the more rigorous lens of academic research. Assigning dollar costs to all corporate activities and impacts, a tenet of full-cost accounting, was found to be a highly subjective exercise. Moreover, attempts to apply traditional accounting methods to nonfinancial transactions were impractical.

Researchers dealing with corporate social responsibility were beginning to make claims about the corporate benefits of stakeholder management and the limitations of the CSR concept. The shift from corporate social responsibility to corporate social responsiveness offered a more secure theoretical foundation. The instrumental argument was made that companies that responded to the interests of their stakeholders in proactive fashion would do better than those who buffered themselves from outside influence. Researchers focused on strategies for managing stakeholder relationships.

At the same time, supply-chain management was receiving considerable attention in the manufacturing trade journals. Numerous case studies documented the bottom-line advantages to companies that developed long-term, highly interdependent relationships with a small group of suppliers. Researchers found that it wasn't just the existence of the relationship that was important, but the qualities of the relationship also mattered. Trust was an essential ingredient for successful, profitable supply-chain relations.

Within the broader management field, I found that the Total Quality Management movement had left an important legacy. First of all, there was the recognition that a relationship with an external stakeholder—the customer—was an important determinant of long-term corporate profitability. Second was the idea that employee teamwork was essential for quality improvement; and third, that every employee had a role to play in building and improving these relationships.

The concept of the learning organization was also important because it looked at the corporation as a system and reinforced the idea that intangible corporate assets such as employee learning and growth could be a source of competitive advantage. Furthermore, it suggested that the capacity of employees to work collaboratively together to learn and innovate was of bottom-line importance especially in flatter, knowledge-based organizations.

The field of community relations was simultaneously undergoing a significant transformation as business leaders recognized the importance of reputation and the strategic value of establishing positive relationships with community stakeholders. More emphasis was being placed on strategic, long-term relationships between companies and nonprofit organizations. Checkbook philanthropy programs were being replaced by cause-related marketing, corporate community investment, and other "win-win" collaborative partnerships.

Many of these partnerships were centered around environmental issues—from recycling to the conservation of habitat for endangered species. Companies that invested in environmental management in the 1980s were working with community groups to expand environmental altruism. Many were also taking a more entrepreneurial tack and finding that by collaborating with other industry or community partners, they could develop innovative solutions to environmental problems and increase profits as well.

At this point, the topic of measuring corporate social performance was beginning to take a back seat in my thinking to the more challenging and immediate issues of how companies establish and maintain collaborative relationships with their stakeholders. Besides the fact that the social auditing area was in its infancy methodologically and theoretically, it seemed to me that a measurement system was only part of the way to consider how companies could maximize the positive impacts they had on stakeholders and minimize the negatives. Furthermore, I believed that to be sustainable in the long term, companies needed to set their own social goals that were integrated with their business strategy. To supersede the nebulous and murky "shoulds" of CSR, there needed to be a win-win solution for both companies and society.

Establishing collaborative relationships had proven beneficial to suppliers, customers, employees, and communities. The convergence of the interests of shareholders and other stakeholders, now that average citizens hold more stocks through their pension plans and mutual funds, simply added force to this argument. While companies and researchers were observing the benefits of stronger relationships in all of these disparate areas, there was no integrated framework for a new approach to management and no practical advice for how companies can build a web of strong stakeholder relationships.

This book is for managers who want to do well and do good but aren't sure how these goals can be accomplished given the undeniable competitiveness and short-term profitability pressures facing companies today. Included are a business case assessment of relationship building, a framework for a new model for corporate-stakeholder relations, and a practical guide for building a profitable web of long-term collaborative stakeholder relationships. The book draws upon recent academic research as well as real-world case studies to illustrate the steps a company can take to develop collaborative stakeholder relationships. It is based on the assumption that while profitability must be ensured, companies have the responsibility and the opportunity to maximize the benefits and minimize the negative impact their actions have on all of their stakeholders, including the natural environment and future generations.

I have come to believe that doing good depends on the expectations that a company has about its stakeholder relationships and the values that shape those expectations. As you will find, the central premise of this book is that corporate social responsibility is about finding "win-win-win" solutions at every turn, about recognizing and building mutually beneficial long-term relationships, and about acting in accordance with a strong set of social and ethical values.

—Ann Svendsen
Vancouver, British Columbia
June 1998

Acknowledgments

More than anyone else, my husband and business partner, Bob Boutilier, deserves credit for the fact that this book was written. Beside providing the financial resources necessary to support us through more than a year of research and writing, he also served as a sounding board for ideas, a hard-nosed critic when necessary, and the primary parent to our two sons as I remained psychologically and physically tied to my desk.

Many others contributed in different ways. I would like to thank Eleonoor Hintzen of Good Company in Holland for her insightful comments on the first draft of the book. I also owe thanks to Elizabeth Godley, whose superb writing and editorial skills were essential during this phase. My partners in CoreRelation Consulting, Kathy Scalzo and Susan Day, also gave encouragement as well as useful feedback as the book took shape. Larry Colero of Crossroads Programs and David VanSeters of the Sustainability Ventures Group shared their ideas and books.

I would also like to thank Myriam Laberge and Don Haythorne of *Breakthroughs* UNLIMITED for sharing their experiences with various organizational transformation methods and Dr. John Waterhouse, Dean of Simon Fraser University School of Business Administration, for his insights concerning both stakeholder contracts and the use of nonfinancial measures of corporate performance.

To my editor, Valerie Barth, publisher Steven Piersanti, and the rest of the folks at Berrett-Koehler Publishers, I send special thanks for believing in collaboration and the viability of this book. Appreciation is also due to Alis Valencia, Carol Goldberg Kirsch, Andrea Markowitz, Richard Weaver, Paul Wright, and Frances Westley for their valuable comments and advice.

Why Build Collaborative Stakeholder Relationships?

To the extent the firm is able to recognize its interdependence, reflect upon the ethical standards appropriate to the situation, and react in a timely and responsive manner, it possesses a valuable, rare and nonsubstitutable strategic resource.

—Reginald Litz, 1996

Companies across North America are taking seriously the notion that as paradoxical as it seems, one way to succeed in a highly competitive globalized economy is to cooperate. In an economy where companies need to persuade investors to hold their stock, employees to work cooperatively with others, customers to buy a broader array of their products and services, and contractors to maintain strong supply chains, collaborative stakeholder relationships are key.

Every company, whether large or small, has a unique set of stakeholders—most often including investors, employees, customers, suppliers, and communities. The term "stakeholders" refers to individuals or groups who can affect or are affected by a corporation's activities.

For most companies today, stakeholder relationships can have a significant impact on the bottom line. While companies could once manufacture an image and reputation through advertising and other media-based campaigns, in today's networked world, reputation depends on establishing the trust of key stakeholders. The pursuit of financial success at the expense of employees, the environment, local communities, or workers in a subcontractor's factory halfway around the globe is not only socially irresponsible but can result in shareholder losses rather than gains.

A growing number of business leaders are acknowledging the power of long-term, positive stakeholder relationships. One such business leader is John Browne, CEO of British Petroleum. In a recent *Harvard Business Review* article (September/October 1997), he talked about the importance of building mutually beneficial stakeholder relationships. He said, "You can't create an enduring business by viewing relationships as a bazaar activity—in which I try to get the best of you and you of me—or in which you pass off as much risk as you can to the other guy. Rather, we must view relationships as a coming together that allows us to do something no other two parties could do—something that makes the pie bigger and is to your advantage and to my advantage."[1]

This is not to say that building stronger relationships with employees, customers, investors, suppliers, and communities is a panacea for all situations or all companies. Nor is building a network of reciprocal relationships simple. In most companies, competitive pressures keep all eyes focused on the short term, making it extremely difficult to bring long-term issues to the forefront. Traditional accounting systems based on financial measures of performance make it difficult to assess the impact of intangibles like relationships or reputation. And collaboration means letting go of control, which is always difficult for corporate managers schooled in the art of competition. However, despite these barriers, for many companies, stakeholder relationships do offer enormous untapped potential. For some, stakeholder relationships may even be a source of competitive advantage.

Stakeholder Collaboration versus Stakeholder Management

The theory of stakeholder management taught in most business schools today focuses on the mechanisms by which organizations understand and respond to the demands of their stakeholders. Theorists have argued that stakeholder relationships can be managed using techniques such as issue analysis, consultation, strategic communications, and formal contracts or agreements. Managers are seen as having the power to direct and control interactions between a corporation and its stakeholders.

The main purpose of stakeholder management is seen to be buffering the organization from the negative impacts of stakeholder activities.

The job of a public affairs or community relations manager, for instance, is to anticipate how the company's activities will affect public stakeholders and minimize negative reactions by instituting "damage control."

Within this more traditional perspective, responsibilities for various stakeholder groups are assigned to separate divisions. The marketing department deals with customer relations, the human resource department deals with employees, the public affairs department deals with the media, the community relations department deals with local organizations, and the purchasing department handles contracts with suppliers. The relationships that develop between managers and stakeholders are shaped by the interests and values of the department managers rather than by the corporation's values and goals.

This "stakeholder management" approach has arisen out of the belief that corporations need to take steps to defend themselves from the demands of stakeholders. Part of the role of managers has been to act as a referee, deftly and diplomatically mediating between stakeholder demands and expectations in order to preserve goodwill toward the company, avoid public relations fiascoes, and maintain cost competitiveness.

Building Stakeholder Relationships

A collaborative approach to building stakeholder relationships, on the other hand, sees stakeholder relationships as being reciprocal, evolving, and mutually defined. The manager is not separate from the stakeholder relationship but is part of it. Thus the idea of "managing" relationships is not only untenable but is viewed as being counterproductive for both the corporation and its stakeholders in the long run.[2]

A collaborative model also assumes that stakeholder relationships can be a source of *opportunity* and competitive advantage. Relationships can increase an organization's stability in a turbulent environment, enhance its control over changing circumstances, and expand its capacity rather than diminish it.

There are significant advantages to taking a more integrated, company-wide approach to identifying and building strategically important stakeholder relationships. In addition to increasing organizational effectiveness and consistency of response, this kind of holistic approach also allows an organization to build on the synergies that occur when positive relationships with one stakeholder group, such as a local community, start to have a beneficial impact on another stakeholder group, such as customers.

The following table summarizes the characteristics of the old and new approaches to corporate-stakeholder relations.

Table 1

Characteristics of Old and New Approaches to Corporate-Stakeholder Relations

Stakeholder Management	Stakeholder Collaboration
fragmented	integrated
focus on managing relationships	focus on building relationships
emphasis on buffering the organization	emphasis on creating opportunities and mutual benefits
linked to short-term business goals	linked to long-term business goals
idiosyncratic implementation dependent on division interests and personal style of manager	coherent approach driven by business goals, mission, values, and corporate strategies

This book presents an integrated strategy for building a network of collaborative stakeholder relationships based on a fundamental shift in management philosophy and attention. A singular focus on the needs and interests of stockholders is replaced by a focus on understanding and balancing the interests of *all* of a company's key stakeholders. Through positive long-term relationships, companies identify "win-win-win" opportunities that serve the corporation as well as stakeholders and society.

The stakeholder strategy is based on the view that companies and society are interdependent. Therefore, business prosperity is linked to the well-being of local and global communities and all of a corporation's other key stakeholders, including employees, suppliers, and the natural environment. Within this context, relationships with stakeholders are as essential to a company's survival as air or water is to a human being's survival.

A company's relationship-building strategy is therefore seen as being inextricably linked to its mission, values, and goals. Given the strategic value assigned to the relationship-building function, employees are expected to act in concert with the corporation's social mission and goals and to identify opportunities that serve the corporation, its stake-holders, and society.

Stakeholder Collaboration on the Ground

Some corporations are already living a "new reality" of collaborative stakeholder relationships. They recognize that positive relationships with stakeholders can pay off. Stakeholder-responsive companies treat their employees and suppliers well, develop innovative products and services, take care of the environment, and contribute to causes that are important to the community. Many find that these stronger stakeholder relation-ships produce benefits ranging from increased customer loyalty to an improved reputation and a more motivated and committed work force.

However, for most companies, the attention of management has been focused on one stakeholder group at a time. Collaborative approaches are often confined to specific parts of an organization. For example, some companies have a participative and democratic approach to employee relations. Others have developed trust-based, highly interdependent rela-tionships with their suppliers and customers. Rare is the company that adopts a comprehensive and strategic approach to relationship building that is governed both by deep social values and by a recognition of the importance of the bottom line.

A number of companies across North America are experimenting with collaboration in some parts of their businesses. If successful, many of these "test cases" will become prototypes for collaborative processes in other areas of these companies.

Case Study: Multistakeholder Collaboration Resolves Decades-Long Dispute

BC Hydro, a utility company in British Columbia, Canada, recently sponsored a successful collaborative process with govern-ment regulators, community action groups, and First Nations (Native American) representatives to develop a new operating plan for a hydroelectric dam on the Allouette River in southwestern BC.

The utility, which produces 90 percent of BC's electrical energy for 1.5 million residential, industrial, and commercial cus-tomers, did not enter the collaborative process willingly. BC Hydro had been fighting with the Allouette River Management Society, a group of concerned citizens, for more than forty years. When BC Hydro announced its plans to increase the generating capacity of the dam, the group threatened to take the utility to court.

Nearby First Nations communities, an active group of naturalists, and regional, provincial, and federal government regulators were also concerned about impacts of the increased water flows on fish habitat, wildlife, and recreation and were prepared to take action. All of these stakeholders had different and conflicting interests.

Under pressure, BC Hydro's multidisciplinary project team, which included engineers, environmental experts, and communications specialists, invited the stakeholders to participate in a collaborative process. For the first time, BC Hydro participated on the committee as an equal player. Over a period of eight months, the committee examined the current operation of the Allouette facility and identified alternatives that would better meet community and environmental needs.

The committee began by developing joint objectives for water management—clearly setting out "what mattered." Government officials, BC Hydro staff, and independent consultants provided information and analysis. They created, evaluated, and re-created various alternatives for operating the facility. Eventually, after months of intense discussions and many rancorous, late night meetings, the stakeholder committee reached consensus on every major aspect of an operating plan.

The benefits of this collaborative process are many. The utility lost some generating capacity but now has a plan that is supported by all of its stakeholders. The river is less prone to flooding and is producing more salmon. The process has also led to further joint ventures between BC Hydro and First Nations groups.

BC Hydro is now using its Allouette River collaborative process as a model for other water-use planning projects. Furthermore, this process has begun to change the corporate mind-set at BC Hydro about how decisions should be made and who should be involved. Many of the members of the staff who participated in the project were initially very skeptical about the merits of a collaborative process that put BC Hydro on equal footing with the other stakeholders. Having been through the very difficult and time-consuming collaborative process, they believe the outcome was worth the effort.

Case Study: Microsoft in Trouble with Stakeholders

Recently, a number of companies have suffered from poor relationships with their stakeholders. Microsoft, one of the world's largest companies, is a case in point. Ironically, Microsoft has been also known as one of the best examples of a networked company— a company that thrives on its stakeholder relationships. That has certainly been the case until recently. Computer hardware and component manufacturers, software developers, and distributors have all collaborated to produce and sell computers that run Windows 95, Microsoft's operating system.

However, as a result of negative publicity arising from its supposed ruthless treatment of suppliers and predatory actions toward competitors, Microsoft is now running into trouble with some of its other stakeholders—the public, investors, government regulators, and employees. There are more than one hundred anti–Bill Gates and Microsoft sites on the Internet.

Company executives report they are having difficulty recruiting new highly skilled employees, and long-time employees are feeling disgruntled and defensive and less motivated to put in the long hours that have been the hallmark of Microsoft and other computer company cultures.[3] As a Microsoft employee wrote recently in Microsoft's on-line public affairs magazine, "A few months ago, everyone I met seemed to think that working for Microsoft was a pretty cool thing to do. Now strangers treat us like we work for Phillip Morris."

In this case, even though Microsoft has succeeded in developing a network of supplier relationships, the strength of those relationships has been undermined by alleged unethical business practices. Furthermore, Microsoft's poor relationships with subcontractors have cost the company the support of at least some of its employees and other key stakeholders.

Case Study: The Body Shop Suffers from Poor Relationships

The Body Shop is another example of a company that has suffered from the lack of solid stakeholder relationships. The Body Shop, one of the world's leading beauty- and bath-products companies, was enormously successful in the early 1990s, riding a wave of public support for its fair-trade and environmental policies. Its success was severely tested several years ago when a media article exposed inaccuracies in the company's environmental and social responsibility claims.[4] The article and the tide of negative consumer and public opinion that followed had a drastic, if short-lived, impact on The Body Shop's stock prices.

When The Body Shop carried out its first social and environment audit in 1995, partly in response to mounting consumer pressure, poor relationships with franchisees and employees also surfaced. Anita Roddick, the founder of The Body Shop, has said in the company's most recent audit report that these relationship problems must be addressed for the company to continue to grow. "We learned in our first social audit process that the overwhelming majority of people associated with our business believe firmly in The Body Shop ideals and our aspirations. We also discovered that a number of improvements were needed in our relationships with stakeholders."[5] Dissatisfied staff and franchise owners, coupled with disenchanted consumers, can put a quick stop to growth and financial prosperity.

Opportunities and Challenges

COMPETITIVENESS PRESSURES

Despite the obvious advantages, in these tough economic times, the idea of stakeholder collaboration can seem a little far-fetched. Many companies face intense pressure to cut costs to the bone just to survive. Global trade, which increased twelve-fold between 1950 and 1995, has intensified competition and the relentless focus of corporate executives on short-term financial performance.[6]

Managers today, for instance, must keep their eyes focused on the bottom line to prevent hostile takeovers. Companies that suffer from declining or even stable stock prices are under threat to be taken over by corporate raiders, stripped of assets, and sold off in pieces. This may mean there is less room for socially responsible corporate initiatives, more centralization of power, less focus on long-term investment, and more attention to the short-term demands of capital markets. Companies are clearly watching the bottom line more closely than ever and are very skittish about the sentiment that they should respond to the interests of non-stockholders.

Global competition also means that corporations are more footloose than ever before. Globalization has increased the size and reach of many corporations and has diminished corporate ties to local communities and even nation-states. Companies that moved from North America to Taiwan or Thailand several years ago are now moving on to Indonesia and China to take advantage of even lower labor costs and environmental standards. This is possible because the Global Agreement on Tariffs and Trade (GATT), which now covers over 90 percent of the world's trade, does not include standards governing workers' rights and environmental protection.[7] Many would argue that the global playing field is no longer level and therefore companies have less incentive to consider other than bottom-line issues.

PUBLIC PRESSURE FOR GREATER CORPORATE SOCIAL RESPONSIBILITY

Corporations do face enormous public pressure to find a balance between the bottom-line interests of their stockholders and broader social responsibilities. Public values are changing. Various studies point to changes in values that have a bearing on what stakeholders want and expect from corporations.

For example, the World Values Survey, a rigorous international study dating back to the 1970s, shows a gradual but significant shift in public opinion. People today are moving away from a concern with material well-being and physical security. In this post-materialist period, quality of life and having input into important decisions are more valued. More people these days also have less confidence in big business. They are less deferential to and more skeptical of authority figures, including business leaders.[8]

Laws have changed in the past two decades in ways that reflect changing public attitudes toward corporate behavior. Since the mid-1980s, for example, laws have been changed in more than thirty states to provide legal protection for boards of directors who resist takeovers that are not in the best interests of employees, suppliers, and community stakeholders. Previously, corporate boards of directors were prohibited from doing other than what was good for stockholders.

A recent review of legal trends in corporate governance indicates that the move toward stakeholder law is not just a United States phenomenon.[9] Germany's recently adopted codetermination laws require employee representation on second-tier boards of directors. Other countries have similarly extended the role of nonstockholders in the governance of corporations. In Denmark, for example, more than fifty large companies have initiated ethical accounting processes where stakeholders are involved in reviewing and rating corporate performance.[10] Through ongoing dialogue, companies aim to align their values and their actions with the values of their stakeholders.

NEW ORGANIZATIONS REQUIRE NEW RELATIONSHIPS

Companies that have been delayered, downsized, hollowed out, and globalized are more dependent on relationships and alliances. Restructured companies depend more on their supply-chain relationships as they outsource noncore functions and create tighter supply relationships. Formerly short-term, arms-length transactions between independent parties are being replaced by long-term partnerships.

Employee relationships are also of growing importance in a knowledge-based economy. Employees must learn from each other and be able and willing to share ideas, even if they come from different backgrounds and cultures. Managers must use stronger relationships with their staff to motivate and inspire rather than use the old chain of command.

While companies today depend on new forms of relationships and partnerships, economic restructuring is making relationship building more difficult. In the post-downsizing era, many employees are tired and overworked. They are doing the jobs of several of their laid-off colleagues in addition to their own and are less willing and able to take on additional tasks that may be perceived as superfluous to the daily grind of meeting their individual sales and production targets.

Economist Jeremy Rifkin in his book *The End of Work* argues that technology and globalization will result in further declines in the demand for labor, causing a weakening of the employee-employer bond, an increase in employee insecurity, a growth in "just in time" contract jobs, and a decline in trust. This is not an environment conducive to relationship building.

A MORE TRANSPARENT ENVIRONMENT

While companies are freer to exploit their competitive advantages worldwide, they are also subject to immediate and powerful public criticism if their behavior falls outside of accepted social norms. Advances in information technology and the fact that average people now have access to inexpensive mass communication channels like the Internet and fax machines makes companies more vulnerable if their actions do not meet public expectations.

Corporate social responsibility receives a great deal of attention now, at least partly because of the increased power of the media to influence public opinion and thereby affect corporate profits. Companies are starting to recognize that to succeed in a networked world where everything about a company can be known instantly, their reputations depend on communicating openly, behaving ethically, and developing credible relationships with their stakeholders and particularly with the communities in which they operate.

Companies are concerned, however, about setting themselves up as "social crusaders" since they may face public criticism if their actions are seen as being self-serving. While the prospect of receiving considerable free publicity for socially responsible business practices is appealing, companies know that if they can't live up to their claims and are not accountable, they risk media attacks, employee dissatisfaction, and a loss of reputation—all of which have repercussions for the bottom line.

While many companies are making great strides in forging credible links with their stakeholders, many business leaders are justifiably cautious. "Companies want to be at the forefront of the rear guard," said David Nitkin, president of EthicScan, a Canadian ethics monitoring company, in a recent speech in Vancouver, Canada.

CYNICISM ABOUT CORPORATE RESPONSIBILITY INITIATIVES

One of the most challenging aspects of the business-community relationship in the 1990s is growing public cynicism. It is no wonder that public faith in big business is at a low point. In the early 1990s as four million jobs were cut in the United States, CEOs' salaries doubled. Executive compensation packages that were tied to stock value grew exponentially, leading average citizens to question the integrity of these business leaders and their commitment to broader social values.

The public is also reacting to corporate "greenwashing." Since the late 1980s, many companies have made unsubstantiated and in many cases false claims about the environmental benefits of their products in attempts to attract customers. Even The Body Shop, an icon of social responsibility, was proven to have exaggerated its claims about recycling and animal protection.

The tarnished reputation and crisis in legitimacy experienced by businesses today is an impediment to relationship building. Scandals like the *Exxon Valdez* oil spill and ongoing conflict over the management of forests have taken their toll on public faith and trust.

CROSS-CULTURAL DIFFERENCES

Members of the public, confronted with the complexities of applying their own culturally defined ethical principles internationally, are also confused about what "corporate social responsibility" really means. Suppliers to several American apparel companies, among them Nike, Inc., and Kmart Corp., are said to have employed children who worked long hours for little pay, in squalid conditions. When these large American companies adopted more stringent requirements for subcontractors, legally hired adolescents were fired with no other viable means of supporting their families. At this point questions arose not only about the acceptability of "sweatshops" but also about the fairness of applying North American ethical codes internationally.

Unfortunately, there is not a one-size-fits-all definition of corporate social responsibility. Ideas about the nature and extent of corporate responsibilities, beyond increasing shareholder profits, vary across cultures, from one historical time period to the next, and even from person to person. In this sense, notions of corporate social responsibility are socially constructed. They are not cast in stone or immutable. Cultural values shape attitudes, which ultimately influence behavior.

Let's look at cross-cultural differences in the relationships between corporations and their stakeholders. These differences reflect varying social and cultural values. For example, within our more individualistic

North American society, more attention has been focused on protecting the interests of stockholders. In other countries, such as postwar Germany, Scandinavia, and Japan, the interests of employees and customers have received more attention.

In Japan, relationships between a business and its suppliers and distributors have always been of central importance. These powerful formal and informal alliances between manufacturers, distributors, retailers, and financial institutions are known as *keiretsu*. *Keiretsu* relationships govern how and with whom business is done among businesses that own each others' stock and sell each others' goods and services. Some theorists, such as Francis Fukuyama in his book *Trust: The Social Virtues and the Creation of Prosperity*, have argued that Japanese firms can establish and maintain such relationships at least partly due to strong cultural values of trust and mutual obligation.

In Germany, Scandinavia, and France, a tradition of stronger collaborative relationships between owners/managers and employees exists. Employee involvement in decision-making, for example, was common in Europe long before it became fashionable in North America. In most European companies, shareholders have less say and workers more say than is common in the United States and Canada.[11]

The fact that we live in an ethnically pluralistic, globalized culture also means that individuals living in the same country may not agree about what corporations should or should not be responsible for or what actually constitutes socially responsible behavior.

For example, the decisions by some large companies, such as Levi Strauss & Co., to give benefits to gay partners of employees and unmarried heterosexual partners may be perceived very differently depending on who is being asked. While this policy may be supported by the majority of employees, customers with strong religious beliefs and others who display less tolerance for homosexuals or unmarried couples may argue that this decision is in fact a socially *irresponsible* business practice.

Similarly, some North Americans may not support initiatives designed to increase diversity in the workplace by giving priority to visible minorities and women in hiring decisions. When stakeholders have conflicting interests and values, which set should the corporation respond to? Whose moral values are sacrosanct?

Globalization adds to the challenge of establishing a workable definition for corporate social responsibility. As Donna Wood, a professor of business administration at the University of Pittsburgh and expert in internal business and society issues, asked recently, "To which society should a multinational enterprise be responsible—home, hosts or all of these? Is a company expected to proselytize for its home country's values? Should it adopt every host country's values? How does the company deal with social change at one or more of its sites? How should managers balance short-term and long-term social expectations among various countries and stakeholders? How do companies assess their responsibilities to the world community rather than to the peoples of various nations?"[12]

A New Approach to Corporate-Stakeholder Relations

It is no wonder that companies, and for that matter the public, are attracted to the concept of corporate social responsibility and uncertain about what it means. Many business leaders and managers, despite wanting to "do the right thing," are unsure where to start. They might agree that building strong, mutually beneficial stakeholder relationships is important, but few understand *how* to establish and maintain win-win associations.

This book presents a new model of corporate-stakeholder relations that helps companies understand how to do well and do good at the same time. The model is based on a North American view of relationships. Corporations and their stakeholders are seen as being engaged in interdependent relationships that evolve and are mutually defined.

These relationships are, however, not without structure. According to the model, they are governed by implicit or explicit "contracts" that define what each party expects from the other and what each is prepared to give. These contracts depend on trust and are subject to ongoing negotiation. Corporate stakeholder strategies are the mechanism by which companies define their expectations and their commitments to stakeholders.

Companies develop these strategies through a rigorous, comprehensive, and interactive process, first by clarifying their own corporate values, then by gathering information about important environmental forces that need to be considered, including information about stakeholder interests. These stakeholder strategies define corporate expectations and commitments, laying out what the corporation wants to achieve and what it intends to do to achieve those goals.

Within the context of this new, more collaborative model of stakeholder relations, rather than ignoring stakeholder demands or attempting to control or direct relationships, managers play a key role in managing the implicit and explicit contracts a company enters into with stakeholders. Managers identify key corporate stakeholders, create opportunities for dialogue, bring an understanding of stakeholder interests and values into corporate planning processes, manage conflicts, and work with stakeholders to identify opportunities for mutual benefit.

What's in This Book

This book presents a new collaborative approach to corporate-stakeholder relations. It is argued that this approach will not only produce positive bottom-line results for corporations operating in our highly competitive, global economy but will also have positive long-term benefits for corporate stakeholders and society in general.

The book includes a business case for collaborative relationships that will be useful to managers who are looking for new ways to build alliances and partnerships and for CEOs or members of boards of directors who are searching for a new strategic approach to managing corporate affairs. A new model of corporate-stakeholder relations provides a framework for understanding why stakeholder relationships are so vital to corporate success and how those relationships can be developed in conjunction with current strategic planning and business management processes.

A six-step guide to the relationship-building process lays out, in easy-to-follow steps, the process that a company goes through to build a network of collaborative stakeholder relationships. The steps are analogous to the process an individual goes through to find a mate—clarifying goals and values, becoming familiar with potential compatible partners, establishing a dialogue, identifying common goals, building trust, and carrying out projects that are mutually beneficial so the relationship lasts.

Readers will find practical tools for aligning their organizations' systems and structures to support relationship building, including an organizational readiness survey, a review of collaboration-friendly communication and information systems, and a description of leading-edge organizational transformation methodologies. These practical tools will help to foster a new awareness of and commitment to relationship building throughout an organization.

The book also provides ideas and strategies for harnessing the power of long-term stakeholder relationships. The book reviews the full range of collaborative relationships, the conditions under which collaboration will be likely to succeed, the challenges involved in collaborative ventures, and the requirements for designing effective collaborative processes, including building trust, resolving conflicts, and communicating effectively.

Finally, via a "stakeholder audit," business leaders will learn how to evaluate the success of their relationship-building initiatives, increasing the depth of their understanding of stakeholders' interests and pointing the way to new opportunities and stronger, more profitable, and sustainable relationships.

Stakeholder Collaboration and the Bottom Line

Products or services are really frozen activities, concrete manifestations of the relationships among actors in a value-creating system.

—R. Normann and R. Ramirez, 1993

This chapter explains why collaboration may be the next source of competitive advantage for many North American companies. We first look at the overall link between corporate social responsibility and profitability and then document the bottom-line benefits of establishing positive relationships with customers, suppliers, employees, and communities and of investing in environmentally sustainable business practices.

Are Socially Responsible Companies More Profitable?

Researchers have been studying the link between corporate social responsibility and profitability for over thirty years. While there is still no definitive answer, most recent studies show that companies that are well managed and have strong stakeholder relationships tend to do better than those who are focused solely on the bottom line.[1]

Research also clearly shows that while stock markets may not always reward companies that are socially responsible, they punish those that are accused of ethical wrongdoing.[2] Evidence shows that following an announcement of a socially irresponsible event, such as an environmental spill or a breach of ethics, a company's stock value goes down significantly. How long prices stay down depends on what the company does to rebuild the trust of its stakeholders.

A recent prize-winning research paper by Sandra Waddock and Samuel Graves from the Boston College Carroll School of Management looks at the link between stakeholder relations, quality of management, and financial performance.[3] Their analysis of the Fortune 500 reputation survey results shows that building positive stakeholder relationships is associated with other positive corporate characteristics. Solid financial performance goes along with good treatment of stakeholders, such as employees, customers, and communities. They also found that companies that treat their stakeholders well are also rated by their peers as having superior management.

The notion that socially responsible companies—those with values beyond the bottom line—outperform other profit-focused organizations was addressed in the book *Corporate Culture and Performance* by Harvard researchers John Kotter and James Heskett. Their study showed that over an eleven-year period, companies that responded to the interests and needs of all of their stakeholders showed four times the growth in sales and eight times the growth in employment of shareholder-focused companies. The authors note that successful companies such as Hewlett-Packard, Wal-Mart, and Dayton Hudson Corp., although very diverse in other ways, share a stakeholder perspective. "All their managers care strongly about people who have a stake in the business—customers, employees, stockholders, suppliers."[4]

A study by Dr. Max Clarkson, director of the Centre for Corporate Social Performance and Ethics at the University of Toronto, indicates that over the longer term, firms that rate highest on ethics and corporate social performance make the most money.[5] Clarkson's research suggests that companies that concentrate exclusively on the bottom line often make poorer decisions, perhaps because they lack the information to anticipate opportunities and to solve problems when they are small and less costly to remedy.

Ethicists and management theorists also insist that ethics are a good business investment. Ethical behavior builds trust, which is a prerequisite for loyalty, innovation, and long-term cooperation. As ethics specialist LaRue Hosmer notes:

> There is a long-term cost to unethical behavior that tends to
> be neglected. The cost is to the trust of the people involved.
> Companies today—due to increasing global competition and

advancing technological complexity—are much more dependent than previously upon the trust of workers, specialists, managers, suppliers, distributors, customers, creditors, owners, local institutions, national governments, venture partners, and international agencies. People in any of those groups who believe they have been misgoverned by bribes, sickened by emissions, or cheated by products, tend, over time, to lose trust in the firm responsible for those actions.[6]

Direct and Indirect Links with Profitability

A corporation's dealings with stakeholders can have a direct as well as an indirect impact on its profitability. For example, companies that can reduce waste in their operations will lower their costs and increase profits. Similarly, companies that ensure their staff behaves ethically will be subject to lower court-imposed fines, and companies that provide a desirable set of benefits for employees will reduce turnover.

Positive stakeholder relationships can also affect profitability indirectly because intangibles like trusting relationships with suppliers, employees' capacity for learning and growth, and a company's reputation and goodwill are key drivers of corporate competitiveness and profitability. For example, environmentally sound business practices can help to create a positive reputation, stronger customer support, and ultimately investor confidence. Companies that establish a positive reputation in a community will find it easier to attract and keep good employees. Employees who feel positive about their jobs and their employer will be more satisfied.

A company's relationship with one stakeholder group, say, employees, can also have a significant impact on several other groups, such as customers and investors. By implementing a comprehensive and internally consistent stakeholder strategy, companies can compound the benefits. Improvements in one stakeholder relationship will undoubtedly create a positive effect on other key relationships and ultimately on bottom-line profits.

In today's knowledge-based economy, stakeholder relationships are especially important to a corporation's financial success and its sustainability in the longer term. Compared with fifty years ago, when corporate assets were primarily machines and other hard assets, today over 60 percent of a company's value is tied up in intangibles like employee know-how, reputation, and trusting relationships with suppliers.[7] Companies that build strong, mutually beneficial relationships with employees, customers, communities, and suppliers create value not only for shareholders but also for these other stakeholders and for society.

A Business Case for Stakeholder Collaboration

Over the past hundred years, we know that strategies for improving profitability have shifted from concrete corporate assets, such as machinery and labor, to intangible assets, such as employee motivation and customer satisfaction. The recently popularized "learning organization" concept heralds a further extension of management's concern into the relatively "soft" area of employee growth and development.

It is not too hard to predict that the next wave of management attention will be on the web of relationships a company has with its external stakeholders and the intangible qualities of those relationships. After all, once a company has re-engineered and restructured the organization for maximum efficiency and effectiveness and has delayered and hollowed out the organization to concentrate on core competencies, relationships take on a much more vital role in ensuring corporate profitability.

The management literature is rife with articles about the benefits of strong supply-chain relationships. Building trusting, mutually beneficial relationships with suppliers reduces costs associated with contracting, monitoring agreements, resolving conflicts, and managing interpersonal dynamics. Such relationships, grounded in mutual interdependence, also serve as incubators for innovation, leading to improvements in quality and product design.

Similarly, research also is beginning to demonstrate what savvy managers have always known—that a company's reputation is as important an asset as bricks and mortar or capital. The rapid growth of the ethical investment market demonstrates the need for companies to be concerned about their social performance.

A company's reputation is also central to its ability to attract new customers and keep existing ones. While a positive reputation is increasingly seen as a source of competitive advantage, the opposite is also true. Corporations whose behavior is judged to be unethical are showered with higher fines, damaging media coverage, and sharp drops in consumer support.

Good relationships with community leaders and organizations in which the company operates are another important source of financial well-being. A company that is viewed as being part of the fabric of the community will be more likely to attract and keep the best employees, reduce costs associated with plant expansions, limit costly government regulations and interventions, and increase support from customers.

Sustainable environmental practices are of course crucial for keeping costs down in the short term and for ensuring that the company is viable in the long term. Concern with environmental issues extends from reducing resource use and thereby costs to developing sustainable business processes to catapult a company into new businesses and new markets.

In the 1980s and early 1990s, the era of public consultation and interest group politics, business leaders came to recognize the importance of managing relationships with local communities, environmentalists, government regulators, and other key stakeholders. They found out, often through painful experience, that they could no longer achieve their goals unless they understood and took account of the interests and needs of those who were affected by their actions.

Today the public and business leaders are looking for new ways to harness the power of business to achieve economic and social goals. In the following sections we look at how and why stakeholder relationships make a difference, beginning with the lifeblood of a corporation—the customers.

Building Relationships with Customers

CUSTOMER PRESSURE—A FORCE TO BE RECKONED WITH

Values held by consumers affect their choices about which companies they do business with. Over the past twenty-five years, the attitudes and values of consumers have changed in ways that differentiate cranky, boycott-happy contemporary customers from their less activist cousins of earlier times.

In the 1980s, customers bought for convenience and sought higher quality at a lower price. Next came the service wave in the late 1980s and early 1990s. Consumers expected improved access to products and services and a quicker response time from the companies involved, as well as personal attention and respect. In response, even the most stalwart firms extended their business hours and offered after-sales support and toll-free information lines.

Management consultant and author John Dalla Costa argues that today's consumers are looking for "wisdom-added" features.[8] They seek connections beyond the transaction, are keen to buy products aligned with their own broader values, and want to make a difference in the world through their spending habits. For these consumers, a company's social performance and demonstrated social vision and values are paramount.

A company's reputation is therefore central to its ability to attract new customers and keep existing ones. Most business people today recognize that an organization's social and ethical values can be a competitive asset. Recent research reinforces the notion that consumers today are more likely to support companies that are actively concerned with social causes and are taking steps to do good while still returning profits to shareholders. A. L. Flood, CEO of the Canadian Imperial Bank of Commerce, said recently, "I think that people are much better informed and they are concerned about things like corporate ethics. And for us to succeed, we must maintain their trust and confidence. Good corporate ethics have to be the foundation of our business."[9]

His views are backed up by a 1996 poll conducted by *Business Week,* which found that 95 percent of adults reject the view that a corporation's only role is to make money.[10] This trend seems to be growing. A 1997 national study of consumer attitudes conducted by Cone/Roper found that 76 percent of consumers would be likely to switch to a brand associated with a good cause, an increase from 63 percent in 1993.[11]

The ability of consumers to affect a company's bottom line through their checkbooks has also been clearly demonstrated in the past decade. Look at the "green" consumer movement, one of the most visible examples of consumers taking action against companies whose policies they disagree with. The recent boycott of Canadian forest companies' products by European consumers has had a serious impact on these corporations' finances and has encouraged some of them to rethink their policies. In fact, Greenpeace and various international wood-product companies in North America and Europe are now working together to come up with product-specific standards. These standards will determine which North American wood products can be effectively marketed in Europe.

A 1995 survey of Canadian consumers by the Market Vision Group indicated that 26 percent of Canadians were actively involved in boycotting goods or services for reasons that had nothing to do with price or quality; the companies were simply viewed as bad corporate citizens.[12] At the top of the list of boycotted companies were tuna companies for endangering dolphins, cosmetics firms for animal testing, and fast food restaurants such as McDonald's Corp. for wasteful packaging.

Numerous publications exist to help these consumers vote with their dollars. *Shopping for a Better World*, published by the U.S. Council on Economic Priorities, and *Shopping with a Conscience*, published by EthicScan in Canada, alert consumers to corporations' records on issues such as gender, diversity, and the environment.

RELATIONSHIP BUILDING: A NEW FOCUS IN MARKETING

There is a renewed focus on relationship building within the field of marketing. Image- and promotion-driven campaigns are being discarded in favor of programs that ensure long-term customer "bonding" and retention. Companies are finding that building long-term relationships with existing customers is easier and five times less costly than finding new ones.

Differentiating products and services based on intangibles such as reputation and quality of relationships is also recognized as a sure way to maintain customer loyalty. Saturn is a good example of a company that is building relationships with its customers and benefiting communities at the same time.

Case Study: Saturn and Its Customers

Saturn, the "alternative" car company, epitomizes a "relationship-driven" approach to marketing and management. Besides believing that their cars are well engineered, designed, and priced, Saturn car owners say they are loyal because of the company's no-haggle policy in showrooms, community involvement, and social values. Saturn's 1994 wildly successful reunion for car owners fostered that feeling of community among the owners. The company has also helped organize local Saturn car clubs, set up an Extended Family Database

on its web site with testimonials from over nine thousand car owners, and organized community events in which Saturn owners,
employees, and affiliates participated—like a recent playground-
building event in Toronto. Materials were donated by local businesses and Saturn owners provided the muscle. The training
received by Saturn retailers (unlike others in the industry, they are
not called dealers) reinforces Saturn's philosophy of teamwork and
the priority given to customer relationship building.

DIALOGUE AND ONE-TO-ONE RELATIONSHIPS

While customer satisfaction is understood to be central to profitability, many corporations lack a deep understanding of what customers
want, why they want it, and how the company can best provide it. These
companies fail to deliver on customer expectations and needs. In other
words, they have not created strong, interactive, mutually beneficial relationships with their customers.

Customer feedback is too often confined to complaint forms and
once-a-year telephone surveys or focus groups. However, companies that
use these limited approaches are losing out to competitors who collect and
remember vital information about individual customer preferences and
use that information to customize products and services and create loyalty. These competitors establish and maintain relationships with their
customers based on two-way dialogue and escalating mutual benefit.
Frequent-flyer programs are a good example of a tool companies can use
to create mutually beneficial, long-term customer relationships.

Leading companies recognize that customer relationships are key to
long-term profitability. Dialogue with customers leads to knowledge that
can be used to customize products and services to meet their customers'
needs, which in turn fosters loyalty, which leads to profits. A case in point
is Levi Strauss & Co., which has saved money and increased loyalty by
customizing jeans for individual customers.[13]

As Don Peppers and Martha Rogers, authors of *Enterprise One to
One*, note, "And when you and your competitor both offer excellent quality product and service, at a fair price, quality itself becomes a commod-
ity. Necessary, but no longer an advantage. More and more, success for
every enterprise will depend on relationship quality—the ability to track
and remember what works for each individual customer."[14]

CAUSE-RELATED MARKETING

Cause-related marketing, which is becoming a very popular marketing tool, involves a long-term partnership between a company and a nonprofit organization. Also known as social marketing, this technique links a corporation's business objectives and marketing resources with initiatives that persuade people to engage in socially beneficial behavior. Some of the earliest social-marketing programs were initiated by governments to encourage exercise, weight reduction, and other healthy behaviors.

A successful example of cause-related marketing undertaken by a company was the Kellogg's All-Bran cereal campaign by Kellogg Co., in collaboration with the National Cancer Institute. This campaign, started in the mid-1980s, encouraged consumers to eat a low-fat, high-fiber diet to reduce the risk of some forms of cancer. The campaign included print and television ads and presentations to health professionals. Some twenty thousand calls to the National Cancer Institute were attributed to the campaign, and the business press reported a significant increase in the sale of All-Bran and other Kellogg cereals.[15]

Many senior executives are enamored with cause-related marketing. In a recent study by Roper Starch Worldwide for Cone Communications, half of the executives surveyed mentioned sales as a major reason to engage in cause marketing. Other more popular reasons included building deeper relationships with customers (93 percent of respondents), enhancing corporate image and reputation (89 percent), and creating or maintaining a compelling corporate purpose (59 percent). As Carol Cone, of Cone Communications, says, "The more sophisticated marketers and positioners understand that a sneaker is just a sneaker is just a sneaker, and a contact lens is just a contact lens, etc. . . . Yes, some of them have brand equity, but more and more it's about what have you done for me lately? What have you done for my community?"[16]

FAIR TRADE—LINKING PRODUCERS AND CONSUMERS

Growing in impact and visibility, fair-trade organizations appeal to consumers' interest in using their purchasing power to support Third World farmers and producers. Fair TradeMark Canada, for example, is organizing a "buycott not a boycott" campaign to encourage coffee drinkers to buy coffee with the TransFair label. In order to use the TransFair label, companies must make credit available for farmers at reasonable rates of interest, offer longer-term purchase agreements, and charge fair prices to reflect the value of farm labor. Started in Holland in 1987, fair-trade organizations now license commercial sales of twenty-four million pounds of coffee beans a year through more than thirteen brand names selling in over thirty-five thousand supermarket outlets.

Other organizations, such as Britain's Traidcraft plc, import and sell a much broader array of fair-traded products including food products, fashions, gifts, and cards and paper. Between 1991 and 1995, Traidcraft experienced a 23 percent increase in the volume of sales to a total of approximately $4.5 million dollars in sales in 1994.

ETHICAL INVESTING

The rapid growth of the ethical-investment market is a further inducement for companies to demonstrate social responsibility. A study by the Social Investment Forum reports that socially responsible investments have jumped 85 percent to $1.185 trillion since 1995 and now account for approximately 9 percent of the $13.7 trillion invested in U.S. funds.[17] In a 1994 study by Walker Research of Indianapolis, 26 percent of potential investors said social responsibility was extremely important in making investment decisions. Investment specialists expect this trend to continue.

A rising number of ethical-investment organizations cater to the interests of both individuals and organizations looking to invest in companies they consider to be socially responsible. Kinder, Lydenberg, Domini, and Co. in the United States and the Social Investment Organization in Canada have devised various criteria to screen out unethical companies. The Domini Social Equity Index, a stock market index of four hundred screened companies, in 1997 posted a three-year annual return of 31 percent as compared to 29 percent for the S&P 500.[18]

Some of the most common criteria or social screens include

- environmental performance
- diversity
- employee relations
- occupational health and safety
- community investment/philanthropy

- international activities/doing business with repressive regimes
- weapon sales or production

Custom-tailored funds are being created: gay rights funds (such as The Meyers Price Value Fund), funds that screen for companies that harm animals (such as Cruelty Free Value), Christian funds (such as Aquinas Equity Growth), and funds that invest according to Islamic principles (such as the Amana Growth Fund).

Progressive ethical investment companies are also looking for companies that are well managed as well as ethical. Investment managers select companies that are profitable and well managed first before applying ethical screens. They aim to select companies that are good stewards of both human and financial capital because if companies are not run efficiently, the market and stockholders will rebel and stakeholders will suffer. They argue that since there is no such thing as a perfectly ethical and socially responsible company, the best they can do is choose companies that balance the interests of all their stakeholders and are also well managed.

The convergence between the interests of shareholders and other stakeholders intensifies the importance of corporate social responsibility to bottom-line success. Most average citizens now have pension funds and own stocks and mutual funds. In fact, institutional shareholders now control 30 percent of corporate equities. Retirees are major shareholders and so are employees, customers, and residents of communities in which companies operate. Often what is good for the community and the company's other stakeholders is also good for shareholders and the bottom line.

Building Relationships with Suppliers

THE IMPORTANCE OF SUPPLY-CHAIN RELATIONSHIPS

In the face of global competition, many companies are forming alliances with suppliers. They are PALing, "pooling, allying, and linking," to use futurist and management consultant Rosabeth Moss Kanter's term. This focus on creating mutually beneficial relationships with suppliers is the focus of "supply-chain management," one of the most popular new concepts in management.

A recent article in the *Journal of Business Strategy* encourages executives from manufacturing firms to establish partnerships with subcontractors to create the kind of interdependencies that currently exist between companies and suppliers in the booming high-tech sector.[19]

Healthy links with both suppliers and customers are especially urgent when custom manufacturing and personalized service are essential for corporate financial survival and when companies are outsourcing non-core functions to become more competitive. Several books have been written recently that deal with the strategic importance of building and maintaining these relationship "webs."[20]

Collaborative relationships between companies in different sectors can also enable companies to leapfrog ahead of their competition. These unique partnerships allow the companies to combine technologies to create products that revolutionize markets. The ability to develop and maintain such relationships is obviously a crucial element in any corporate strategy.

TRUST LINKED TO LOWER COSTS

Recent research explains why establishing trusting, cooperative relationships with stakeholders positively affects a company's financial performance and can produce a significant competitive advantage.[21] Findings have been compiled from stakeholder theory, economics, behavioral science, and ethics. The basis of the argument is the notion that a firm is a nexus of formal and informal contractual relationships that exist between it and its stakeholders.

Senior executives contract with stakeholders, either directly or indirectly through their managers. Because the contracting process can be affected by problems associated with commitment such as agreements on costs, interpersonal dynamics, adherence to schedules, and so on, firms that can solve these problems efficiently will save money.

When firms and their suppliers trust each other, the costs of monitoring and managing contracts are lower. Companies experience less conflict with their suppliers, resulting in fewer legal suits, and there is a heightened capacity for innovation. These firms will have a competitive advantage over firms that do not have trusting relationships, all else being equal. This is an important observation, given the strategic importance of supply-chain links and the growing number of these relationships a company must manage.

Case Studies: The Benefits of Interdependence

The trend toward tighter bonds between manufacturing companies and their key suppliers was the focus of a recent article in *Industry Week*.[22] The article profiled two fast-growing companies, Motoman, Inc., and Stillwater Technologies Inc., that have developed a tightly integrated and highly successful collaborative relationship. Motoman, Inc., a leading supplier of industrial robotics systems, and Stillwater Technologies Inc., a contract tooling and machining company, now occupy offices and manufacturing space in the same facility. Their telephone and computer systems are linked, and they share a common lobby, a conference room, and an employee cafeteria.

The ties between the two companies developed over several years. Initially, Stillwater performed relatively small contracts for Motoman. Trust developed as senior employees moved between the two organizations. An expansion in Motoman's operations led to a proposal to Stillwater to share space. This closer proximity eventually led to more information sharing, joint projects, and new opportunities. Executives from both companies attribute their continued success to their ability to collaborate effectively.

The article noted that supplier firms are also locating next door to their large customers, and in a relatively few cases, such as at the Volkswagen Do Brasil plant in South America, suppliers have installed themselves in their customers' plants and are carrying out some of the production work. The owners of the larger companies have found that collaborative partnerships with their suppliers are helping to reduce costs and improve the design and overall quality of products. These kinds of partnerships also allow for greater specialization, more flexibility, and improved competitiveness in a globalized economy.

However, according to the authors of the article and other experts in the field of business-to-business collaboration, a key to making these strategic alliances work is relationship management—having the expertise, processes, and philosophies needed to establish and sustain relationships. An essential element underlying relationship building is, of course, trust.

According to an article in *Harvard Business Review*,[23] IKEA, a Swedish retailer of home furnishings, has been successful because it has "systematically redefined the roles, relationships, and organizational practices of the furniture business." According to authors Richard Normann and Rafael Ramirez, IKEA's ability to build and maintain strong relationships with customers and suppliers is fundamental.

For example, IKEA emphasizes finding and training the right suppliers, commits to long-term relationships, and helps suppliers improve their products by leasing them equipment, providing technical assistance, and helping source raw materials.

Building Relationships with Communities

FROM CORPORATE PHILANTHROPY TO CORPORATE SOCIAL INVESTING

Public views about corporate responsibilities beyond profit making have evolved over the past several decades. Until the 1950s, companies were legally prohibited from making donations or otherwise getting involved in community affairs.

However, in the late 1960s, the U.S. public began demanding that corporations donate some of their profits to social causes. In response to this pressure for greater corporate social responsibility, most companies set up "arm's-length" foundations to dispense money—up to 5 percent of pretax profits in some cases. However, the interests of society were considered best met if the philanthropic donations of companies were not aligned with their business goals.

Most companies took great pains to ensure their giving programs were unfettered by corporate business interests. Financial institutions supported the arts, small retailers supported amateur sports, and industrialists gave to hospitals. The United Way was established as a clearinghouse for public donations to small charities, and its major source of revenue came from employee fund-raising campaigns. Few companies established criteria for their philanthropy and gave small amounts to numerous charities.

The late 1970s and 1980s can be characterized as a time of low demands for corporate social responsibility or accountability. Many look back on this period as one of unconstrained greed, as companies whose share values were stagnant or in decline were taken over, stripped of assets, and sold in pieces.

In the early 1990s, however, public attitudes shifted again, at least partly in response to the seemingly unbridled acquisitiveness of companies in the 1980s. The public again expressed its concern that business was not adequately responding to community needs and should be more involved in solving mounting social problems. Companies began to take a more active role in tackling social problems. In the early 1990s, the Business Roundtable in the United States echoed this view when it stated that business should "serve the public interest as well as private profits."

This change in public values is reflected in recent amendments to corporate governance laws. Statutes have been adopted recently in at least half of the states in the United States that extend the range of permissible concern by boards of directors to a host of nonshareholder constituencies, including employees, creditors, suppliers, customers, and local communities. Recent court decisions have allowed directors to include factors such as long-range business plans and a corporation's "culture" in their decision making.

Today, companies are investing in longer-term relationships with community-based organizations because they see significant benefits of stronger community ties, including the ability to attract and retain highly skilled workers, improvements in employee morale, and increased customer loyalty and support.

Companies are also responding to intense public pressure to deal with social problems in the wake of government cutbacks. To cope with simultaneously declining community-relations budgets, businesses are attempting to leverage their contributions by working collaboratively with others, by contributing time instead of dollars, and in some cases by taking on an advocacy role to vocally support a community cause. Multiparty partnerships and other collaborative processes are being more widely used to resolve social problems.

Companies are also taking a closer look at how their business decisions affect community stakeholders and are searching for opportunities to create win-win outcomes. Some of the major areas where businesses have recognized they can have a positive impact on communities include site location; investment in capital facilities; site revitalization; human resource policies such as hiring, job creation, and training; and contracts with minority firms.

CORPORATIONS AND COMMUNITY ECONOMIC DEVELOPMENT

Community economic development (CED) initiatives led by local organizations that mobilize resources for a multifaceted development campaign are also gathering momentum. Corporate support for community development grew from $8 million given by 8 corporations in 1987 to $23 million given by 282 corporations in 1991 according to a study by the Council for Community Based Development.[24]

Rather than taking the lead, corporations usually participate as members of a CED campaign directed by local organizations and community leaders. Their participation can range from direct investment to contributions of volunteer time, training and strategic planning support, revolving loan funds, or grants and donations.

According to a recent Conference Board of Canada study, CED can help a corporation "expand its customer base and revenue, build and retain market share, meet its staff development needs, gain access to skilled labor, or enhance its reputation with customers, investors, government and regulators."[25]

The following are some examples of recent community investment initiatives undertaken by North American companies.

> **Case Studies:** Corporations and Communities
>
> America Business Collaboration for Quality Dependent Care (ABC) is a consortium of twenty-two companies that have made a six-year commitment to raise $100 million to improve child and elder care in communities where they operate. The program is called "Teach Plus," and the money supports teacher training and curriculum development in community care centers. The aim of the initiative is to produce better caregivers who stay longer in their jobs.[26]
>
> Seafirst Bank has formed partnerships with Indian Nations in Washington State to support tribal economic development through business education, employment development, and lending. Seafirst helped develop a series of education programs to provide

the skills and knowledge needed for personal financial management and tribal economic development, encouraged children's interest in science through a festival in 1995, developed a curriculum for Native Americans at Northwest Indian College, and provided training for Seafirst employees to better understand Native American cultural issues central to building business relationships with this community.

Royal Dutch/Shell, vilified in the media in the past for investments in repressive regimes and for its mishandling of the Brent/Spar oil rig platform disposal, has recently made some dramatic changes in the way it deals with its external stakeholders in an effort to rebuild its reputation and improve its operations. The company has invited representatives from environmental and human rights groups to participate in internal business meetings and to monitor the company's most sensitive initiatives. Senior managers believe that the scrutiny of nongovernmental organizations will strengthen their performance and turn what was once an adversarial relationship into a mutually beneficial one for both the environmental community and the company.

Building Relationships with Employees

Most business leaders recognize that a healthy bottom line depends on establishing positive employee relationships. Good employee relations can mean a decline in absenteeism, fewer days lost to strikes, greater capacity for innovation, and more efficient operations. Staff-responsive initiatives can also help companies attract and keep valued employees.

Recognizing the importance of creating a "partnership" with their employees, companies have installed benefits packages, policies, and programs designed to help employees cope with responsibilities outside of work. As the workforce has become more diverse, human-resource policies have become more inclusive. In short, over the past decade corporations have made great strides in responding to the needs of employees by putting in place policies that prevent discrimination and support employees as they cope with the demands of the new economy.

Beyond job-related policies, some companies have also created new ownership and decision-making structures that substantially alter the relationship with employees. Employees are involved in ownership through stock options, employee stock ownership plans (ESOPs), participatory decision making, and profit-sharing plans.

In "flatter," less hierarchical organizations, employees must work more collaboratively with others inside and outside the company. Employee teams are expected to be more creative and agile, able to respond rapidly to meet evolving customer needs. With no time for formality, relationships based on trust and mutuality rather than authority and power are fundamentally important.

While high-powered collaborative work teams are the exception rather than the rule, the first step toward such "breakthrough" groups is assuring employees that their values, goals, and perspectives are understood and taken into account by others. This can go a long way toward healing the breach between the existing levels of dissatisfaction among employees and the kind of dynamic, relationship-based organizations of the future.

RELATIONSHIPS: A SOURCE OF ORGANIZATIONAL STRENGTH

A company's stakeholder relationships can be a source of organizational strength, as Richard Barrett, formerly the values coordinator at the World Bank, found when he examined the values of eighteen highly successful companies.[27] All of these companies had a strong core ideology of nurturing the well-being of the organization and its people. Maximizing shareholder wealth was not the prime organizational goal.

A focus on values gave meaning to employees' lives, and they experienced a shift in attitude from "what's in it for me/us?" to "what's best for the common good?" Barrett argues that companies whose employees share a common purpose beyond making money can "tap into (their) human potential . . . as emotional, not mental energy, is the motivator of the human spirit."

A good reputation helps companies attract and keep good employees, which is in turn expected to provide companies with the greatest single source of competitive advantage in the coming decade. Diverse, mobile, and highly skilled workers care about the ethical reputation of the companies they work for. They also stay where they are valued and where they can learn and grow. To succeed in the new knowledge economy, companies will need to develop and demonstrate strong corporate social values and create work environments that support innovation and collaboration.

A recent survey of 2,100 MBA students showed that more than half of the respondents would accept a lower salary to work for a socially responsible company. Two-thirds said they would take a 5 percent cut in pay; the other third said they would take a 10 percent cut or more.[28]

Management specialists have also found that when employees are treated well, they are more apt to treat customers well and to put the long term interests of the corporation ahead of their own self-interests. The link between employee satisfaction and customer satisfaction demonstrated in a recent Northern Telecommunications' study provided a solid business case for the company's extensive programs to improve employee health, safety, and well-being.

Case Studies: The Benefits of Employee Collaboration

BankBoston recently instituted an innovative transition program for employees in an effort to mitigate the impacts of its layoff of two thousand people resulting from its merger with BayBank Inc. BankBoston's Transition Assistance Program offers a six-month stipend at $10 per hour for up to twenty hours per week to employees who go to work for a nonprofit organization, three months' salary at $15 an hour for up to forty hours a week at any nonprofit company that is not a competitor with the bank, internships with noncompeting employers, job retraining, and small business loans for those who want to start their own businesses.[29]

San Jose National Bank reduced turnover and the use of consultants by allowing new mothers to bring babies to work up to the age of six months. First Tennessee Bank found that units run by managers who ranked highest in the "work and family" area, as measured by employee surveys, have a 7 percent higher customer-retention rate.[30]

Dana Corp. has developed an effective suggestion program. It holds classes in "drumming up better ideas" and offers awards, luncheons, and other forms of recognition as incentives. Each business unit runs its own suggestion program, and the company reports that 70 percent of ideas are put into effect.[31]

The Environment as Stakeholder

Most businesses in the 1960s and even 1970s ignored the natural and physical environment or at best viewed it as a fairly remote influence on decision making. The externalized environmental and social costs of corporate activities were largely unacknowledged. Companies used "end of the pipe" solutions to pollution. Then came a series of environmental disasters: Love Canal in 1976, Three-Mile Island in 1979, Bhopal (India) in 1984, and Chernobyl in 1986. These environmental crises led to a rising tide of public fears and concerns and a tightening of legislation governing corporate environmental behavior.

In the early 1980s, most large industrial companies set up environmental-management departments to manage environmental problems through pollution abatement and waste-reduction programs. Widespread business interest in the relationship between corporate well-being and the physical environment surfaced in the late 1980s with the publication of *Our Common Future* written by Gro Bruntland for the World Commission on Environment and Development. The idea that economic development depended on a healthy environment was taken to heart by business leaders.

In many companies, concern about the environment has since moved from the line department into the boardroom. Environmental issues are now reflected in a company's mission as well as in marketing and management strategies. A recent *Harvard Business Review* article by Stuart Hart, "Beyond Greening: Strategies for a Sustainable World,"[32] shows how corporate environmental policies and practices have changed over the years. Many companies now accept that they have a responsibility to do no harm to the environment, and some have found they can increase profits if they reduce pollution levels and minimize the consumption of resources. They have moved from pollution control to pollution prevention.

Leading companies today are going even further to adopt a "stewardship" philosophy of environment management. This means taking responsibility not only for minimizing direct impact on the environment but also for reducing impacts associated with the full life cycle of their companies' products. Looking beyond the physical and temporal boundaries of their corporations, these leaders understand and take account of the physical and social costs of doing business. They ask themselves how their companies need to change to ensure future sustainability, and they develop new sources of information, ideas, and relationships to help their companies along that path.

Hart describes the recent efforts by Monsanto Co., one of the world's largest chemical companies, to redirect its agriculture business from bulk chemicals to biotechnology, expecting that bioengineering of crops will be a more sustainable strategy for increasing agricultural yields as compared with the application of chemical pesticides or fertilizers.

ENVIROPRENEURIALISM—PARTNERSHIPS FOR SUSTAINABILITY AND PROFITS

The perception that there is an inherent trade-off between protecting the environment and corporate profitability still persists. However, a just-released report by the World Business Council for Sustainable Development counters this perception and shows that companies that rate highly for environmental performance yield better-than-average returns to shareholders.[33]

In fact, whole new industries are being created by "enviropreneurial marketers," who are developing environmentally friendly products that allow them to meet a consumer need and at the same time satisfy society's interest in protecting the environment.[34]

Rather than chipping away at the profit margin, increasing environmental standards can trigger innovations that lower the total cost of a product or improve its value. Management theorists argue that the more strategic the environmental innovation, the greater the potential for developing, maintaining, and enhancing a sustainable competitive advantage. This is because these strategies will be rare and difficult to imitate because they will be unique to the organization.

More companies are beginning to focus on developing sustainable technologies and practices and in some cases are developing new, more sustainable areas of business in the process. John Browne, the CEO of British Petroleum, for example, recently announced that his company will focus on the development of renewable energy resources because of the threat of global warming and the likelihood that the use of petroleum-based fuels may be heavily regulated in the future. Interface Inc. has also embarked on a major campaign toward sustainability.

Case Study: Interface Rethinks the Carpet Business

After reading Paul Hawken's book *The Ecology of Commerce*, which left him feeling "convicted in my heart," Ray Anderson decided to turn his company into "the first sustainable industrial enterprise in the world."[35] Interface, with five thousand employees worldwide, converts petrochemically derived materials into carpets, carpet tiles, and fabrics. Anderson first developed a program called "EcoSense" to eliminate waste from the company's operations by reducing nylon use with a new tufting method, recycling fibers, replacing nonrenewable materials, treating water for irrigation purposes, and utilizing a gravity-feed energy system.

He then reconceptualized the carpet manufacturing business as a "carpet leasing" and recycling venture. Interface now produces carpet tiles that it leases to companies. When the tiles are worn out, Interface removes them, recycles the materials, and replaces the tiles. Anderson stresses that his company's strategy makes economic as well as social sense. "I really think there's a new paradigm emerging," he says. "Folks, we're in the business to do well. And we can do well by doing good. And by doing good we set an example that attracts other people to the game."

According to a recent article in the *Wall Street Journal* (July 1, 1997), these measures have saved Interface $25 million since 1995, with another $50 million expected in the next two years.

ENVIRONMENTALISM AND THE MOVEMENT TOWARD STAKEHOLDER COLLABORATION

How do the sustainability literature and the "environmental revolution" help us understand the movement toward more collaborative approaches to stakeholder relations? First, in addition to the moral and ethical imperative, the environmental sustainability movement has clearly demonstrated why paying attention to how companies affect the environment makes good business sense. Experience shows that nonpolluting, resource-conserving companies tend to be more profitable. The same argument can be made for companies that pay attention to their other stakeholders.

Second, environmentalists and others have been some of the first to describe the interdependence that exists between businesses and the environment and to argue that business has a major role to play in ensuring society's sustainability. The late futurist Willis Harman argued that "Business has become in this last half-century the most powerful institution on the planet. The dominant institution in any society needs to take responsibility for the whole."[36] Building on the notion of environmental stewardship, companies are reminded of the important role they have to play in global social and ecological sustainability.

Third, many involved in the sustainability movement have made the case that individual business leaders must undergo a profound transformation in their personal values away from the technocentric views of past years toward a more spiritually connected, future-oriented view of the world.[37] When executives apply that new perspective to their businesses, they may, like Ray Anderson, CEO of Interface Inc., ask tough questions about how sustainable their businesses are and, further, what they need to do to change their companies to create benefits for all of their stakeholders and society.

Finally, as you will see from the following case examples, one of the hallmarks of "enviropreneurialism" is collaboration—among business units, suppliers, customers, and even competitors.

Case Studies: Collaborating to Solve Environmental Problems

CP Rail, a large Canadian transportation company, recently responded to the challenge of keeping rail-bed weeds under control without herbicides. It started looking for less-harmful solutions that would be both cost effective and acceptable to the citizens of communities straddling the railway tracks.

After an enterprising employee suggested using steam to kill weeds, the company invested the dollars and the time to develop a prototype steam machine. Not only did this innovation put an end to protesters flinging their bodies in front of trains and to reams of negative media coverage, the steam machine saved the company money in chemical costs, reduced environmental impact to zero, and created very positive community and media relations. The use of steam also circumvented tightening government herbicide regulations. CP even thought about selling the machine to other railroad companies for a profit, although it eventually did not pursue this idea. However, one potential barrier to the continued use of the steam machine has arisen: the weeds have adapted to the steam treatment, causing CP Rail to once again search for a solution.

An article in *Industry Week* magazine (January 1997) describes an innovative partnership between Maytag Corp. and the Electric Power Research Institute (EPRI). The two organizations collaborated on research and development (R&D) to develop a new energy-efficient washing machine. The joint R&D served the needs of both organizations. Maytag wanted to develop a new washer that would appeal to energy-conscious consumers, and the EPRI was interested in the project because it would help reduce demand for electricity and ultimately benefit member utility companies. Both organizations were sold on the idea of keeping costs down and the quality of research high.

EPRI provided money for the R&D, and Maytag did the development work. As part of the R&D process, they created an advisory panel of outside experts and other stakeholders, including state and regional government regulators and potential customers. The panel provided input on marketing and product design. EPRI also undertook a marketing program to support the launch of the new washer, which included an energy-efficient, horizontal-axis design, and offered $150 to anyone purchasing one.

This collaborative venture is instructive for several reasons. First, the groups collaborated on tasks that were formerly seen in strictly competitive terms. Second, they identified consumer trends and took steps to meet an emerging consumer need through the collaborative R&D project. Third, they sought input from other stakeholders in the process, and fourth, the R&D project has led to a longer-term relationship between the two organizations and with it, further opportunities.

DuPont's sustainable business practices were profiled in a recent cover story in the *Green Business Letter* (October 1997). The company has reduced material use, created closed-loop systems, turned waste streams into profitable businesses, and invented new business relationships with its customers. It also has developed sulfonylurea, a herbicide that uses 1/100 of the volume of conventional chemicals, making it less toxic and cheaper for farmers to use with no decrease in crop yield. These initiatives have all contributed to increased revenue for the company.

Eco-Trust, a six-year-old Oregon-based environmental organization, focuses on collaboration with businesses to protect the environment (*USA Today*, September 1997). Eco-Trust works with local communities in the Pacific Northwest to identify projects that help to build the local economy and protect the environment. The group is trying to establish Green Bank to lend money to "green entrepreneurs and support environmentally friendly developers." Wells Fargo Bank contributed $1 million and Weyerhaeuser Co. contributed to a revolving loan fund.

A Model for Corporate-Stakeholder Relations

All human motivations are based on self-interest. We are only moti-
vated to do something when it benefits us in some way. What about
the common good? Are actions that support the common good also
based on self-interest? Yes, but . . . it is a self with an enlarged sense
of identity. It is a self that identifies with family, community, the
organization it works for, society and the planet. It is a self that rec-
ognizes that it is part of a web of interconnectedness that links all
humanity and living systems. In management terminology it is a
self with a systems perspective. In spiritual terminology it is a self
that is in touch with its soul.

—Richard Barrett, 1998

This chapter presents a new model of corporate-stakeholder relations. The model, which covers the cycle of corporate activity from research and strategy development to the design and implementation of business processes, illustrates the ways in which stakeholders and stakeholder relationships influence corporate activity. (See figure 1.)

The model is based on a systems view of corporations in society and the idea that companies are engaged, whether actively or passively, in relationships with their stakeholders. Corporate-stakeholder relationships are seen as evolving, mutually defined, and governed by implicit and explicit contracts. These contracts, which are often unspoken and subjected to ongoing negotiation, specify what both parties expect from the relationship and what they will give in return.

Stakeholder relationships are seen as being the lifeblood of the organization. Just as other living entities exist in a symbiotic relationship with their environment, so do corporations. Stakeholder relationships provide the energy, information, and resources that are necessary for survival. Through these relationships a company creates social, intellectual, environmental, and financial capital—all essential to long-term sustainability and growth.

Following an explanation of key elements of the model, several ideas from systems theory are explored in more detail, and finally, a case study is presented to further illustrate the model.

A Contracting Framework

Corporations have been defined as a "nexus of contracts."[1] These contracts specify or imply what the organization expects from each stakeholder group to help it achieve its primary objectives and what each stakeholder expects from the organization in return for its cooperation.[2] Within this contracting framework, one of the most important managerial functions is to establish and maintain stakeholder relationships.

Contracts can be either explicit or implicit. Explicit contracts, such as collective agreements or supplier contracts, are enforceable by law. Implicit contracts are those in which obligations or deliverables cannot be precisely specified in advance. They are not enforceable by law as the results are difficult to observe and judgments about the value of each party's contributions are subjective. Implicit contracts are sometimes referred to as "self-enforcing" contracts[3] or "relational" contracts.[4]

A company may have multiple contracts with a given stakeholder group. It may, for example, expect to provide its employees with wages, benefits, and job security in exchange for specialized skills. These expectations may be written down in explicit employment contracts. Companies may also establish implicit contracts with their employees, for example, about ethical behavior or willingness to put in overtime when asked. Though unspoken, these implicit contracts define expectations and affect behavior and therefore the relationships that exist between the parties.

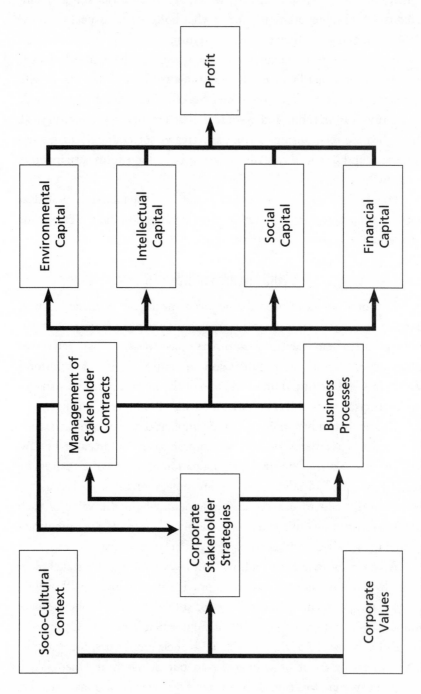

Figure 1. A Model of Corporate–Stakeholder Relations

Companies also have implicit and explicit contracts with customers, suppliers, and communities. Customers, for example, provide resources in exchange for products or services. Communities grant a company the right to build and operate facilities in exchange for tax payments and the provision of local employment. Customers may expect that products will be defect free or produced using environmentally sound methods. If the company meets those expectations, the customer-company relationship will flourish. If not, the customer will be dissatisfied, and the relationship may be terminated.

Implicit contracts exist and are sustained when both parties benefit from having a long-term relationship and both need the flexibility that such a contract offers. Implicit contracts, because they are informal, rely heavily on reputation and trustworthiness to ensure compliance.

Within this contracting framework, corporate-stakeholder relationships are understood to be reciprocal and mutually defined. Companies don't "manage" their stakeholder relationships, but rather manage their expectations of the relationships and their decisions about what they will do to sustain them.

DEVELOPING STRATEGY FROM A STAKEHOLDER PERSPECTIVE

Normally, the strategy-development process begins when corporate executives identify customer requirements and then consider the requirements and potential contributions of employees, suppliers, and other key stakeholders. The company chooses a set of strategies that reflect and support its web of stakeholder relationships and the implicit and explicit contracts it has with its stakeholders.

To be effective, a strategy must take account of information the organization receives from the external environment, including information about stakeholder interests and values. For example, if customer satisfaction is identified as a strategically important goal, the strategy must address the question of what creates customer satisfaction. Companies must know what customers want.

Strategies also reflect corporate values. A company's core values, whether clearly articulated or not, influence the selection of strategic goals and decisions about how the company will negotiate and carry out its explicit and implicit contracts with stakeholders.

Finally, the strategy identifies which stakeholders are important to a corporation's success and why. Stakeholders may be important because they contribute to profitability, because corporate management and the board feel a sense of social responsibility to the stakeholder group, or because the corporation is legally obligated to attend to that stakeholder group.

American companies, for example, are required by law to protect the safety and health of employees. Measures designed to ensure employees' health and safety are often incorporated into corporate strategy. The same is true of legal requirements to protect the environment. Given that employee satisfaction is linked to customer satisfaction, which ultimately affects profitability, many companies also include customers as well as employees in their strategies. Lastly, the more indirect but still important link between corporate reputation and profitability is leading many companies to include communities and other external stakeholders in their strategies.

FINANCIAL, SOCIAL, INTELLECTUAL, AND ENVIRONMENTAL CAPITAL

The final major element of the model relates to the outcome of corporate activity. As the World Bank and Skandia, a Swedish financial services company, have argued recently, companies generate intellectual, environmental, and social capital in addition to financial capital.[5]

Financial capital is obviously created by the sale of products and services to customers. Intellectual capital is generated through activities that increase employee capacity for learning and the capacity of the organization to meet customer and market requirements. Environmental capital is created through proper environmental management and the reduction of emissions and waste. Social capital is created through positive interactions between the company and its stakeholders. The more trusting the relationships, the more social capital is created.

The model assumes that corporate performance can be measured using a stakeholder audit that incorporates nonfinancial as well as financial measures. A stakeholder audit allows corporations to begin to track and therefore understand the impact of stakeholder relationships on bottom-line success. (See chapter 10 for a full discussion of stakeholder audits.)

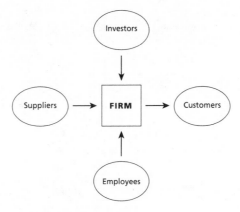

Figure 2. Input-Output model of the corporation

Source: Tom Donaldson, "The Stakeholder Theory of the Corporation: Concepts, Evidence and Implications," *Academy of Management Review* 20, no. 1 (1995): 65-91.

Systems Theory and Corporate-Stakeholder Relations

Corporations today operate in an increasingly boundaryless world in which information and relationships are both more important and more fluid. These new conditions require a theoretical framework that is equally dynamic. Unfortunately, existing static theories of the corporation do not meet this challenge.

We see, when looking back several decades, that our theories initially treated corporations as separate from society. The "input-output" model that was taught in introductory business management courses until the mid-1980s, for example, is based on the idea that suppliers, investors, and employees provide "inputs" to a firm that are transformed into "outputs" such as products and services for customers. Suppliers provide inputs to the firm, and customers consume the outputs of corporate activity. In this mechanistic model, seen in figure 2, two-way links between the firm and its stakeholders do not exist.

STAKEHOLDER THEORY

About twenty years ago, a new theory emerged that was based on the idea that corporations and society are "interpenetrating systems." One of the earliest proponents of what is known as stakeholder theory was R. E. Freeman, who wrote *Strategic Management: A Stakeholder Approach*. He

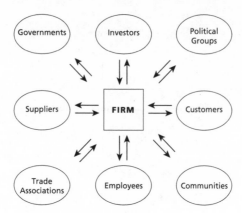

Figure 3. The stakeholder model of the corporation
Source: Tom Donaldson, "The Stakeholder Theory of the Corporation: Concepts, Evidence and Implications," *Academy of Management Review* 20, no. 1 (1995): 65-91.

argued that each company has its own unique set of stakeholder groups who are affected by corporate activities and can affect the corporation.

A company's primary stakeholders are those groups whose interests are directly linked to the fortunes of the company—typically shareholders and investors, employees, customers, suppliers, and residents of the communities where the company operates. The natural environment, nonhuman species, and future generations are also seen as primary stakeholders in that corporate activities can have a direct impact on them.

Secondary stakeholders include those who can indirectly influence a corporation or who are less directly affected by its activities. They are not directly engaged in transactions with the corporation and are not essential for its survival. The media and pressure groups are defined as secondary stakeholders, since they can affect the reputation of a company by mobilizing public opinion in support of or against corporate activities.

Stakeholder theory is still evolving.[6] Researchers, for example, are still debating which stakeholders a company ought to deal with. Some researchers take a normative perspective arguing that companies *should be* more socially responsible because it's the right thing to do. This line of research has been inconclusive, mostly because no one can agree on what constitutes socially responsible behavior. It depends, naturally, on who is doing the judging.

Others focus on the "instrumental" value of stakeholder relations, attempting to understand how managers actually handle stakeholder claims. The three main characteristics of stakeholders that determine

Table 2.
The Evolution of Corporate-Stakeholder Theory

Theory of Corporations	Corporation's Relationship to Society	Responsibility of Corporation	Role of Managers	Management Style
Input-Output	independent	to make a profit	agents of shareholders	defensive
Stakeholder	interpenetrating	to respond to stakeholders	relationship managers	buffering
Systems	interdependent	to find ethical, "win-win" opportunities with stakeholders	stewards, relationship builders	collaborative

their salience or importance for managers, according to Ronald Mitchell from the University of Victoria, are their legitimacy, their power, and the urgency of their claims.[7]

The first characteristic of stakeholders is legitimacy. Does the group have a moral or ethical or legal claim on the corporation? The second characteristic is power. Does the stakeholder group have the power to affect the corporation? The third is the degree of urgency that the group or individual represents. Is the stakeholder making a claim for urgent action? Is the group demanding immediate attention from the corporation? The authors argue that these three characteristics influence whether a manager will pay attention to the stakeholder group or not.

A SYSTEMS VIEW OF THE CORPORATION

While most business leaders today accept the idea that companies have "stakeholders" that both affect the organization and are affected by it, the dynamism of the relationship and the degree of interdependence between companies and their stakeholders is less widely understood.

As you can see in table 2, our views about the nature of the links between corporations and society have evolved. Some would argue that we are again on the threshold of a major shift in perspective from a stakeholder theory to a systems-based theory of corporations in society.

A systems-based theory assumes that the corporation is embedded in a network of interdependent stakeholder relationships that are evolving and mutually defined. Thomas Donaldson and Lee Preston, two of the leading stakeholder theorists, define corporations as "a network involving multiple participants and interests, each of which may make contributions and receive rewards as a result of corporate activity."[8]

This more dynamic view of corporate-stakeholder relations acknowledges the interdependence that exists between companies and their stakeholders and asserts that stakeholder relationships can be a source of opportunity and competitive advantage rather than simply a threat or a drain on corporate resources.

James Moore, in his recent book *The Death of Competition*,[9] coins the term "business ecosystem" to denote the network of reciprocal, mutually beneficial relationships that define a company and provide a source of growth and renewal. The business ecosystem for a restaurant in a small community, for example, could include its relationships with the local sports team that it sponsors, the high school that provides a labor pool, the agency that provides utilities, and the government to which the restaurant pays its taxes.

A business' ecosystem consists of multiple stakeholder relationships. Within that business ecosystem, corporate decision makers and stakeholders cooperate, compete, and co-evolve, as each develops new capabilities and forces others to grow and change.

THE IMPLICATIONS OF SYSTEMS THEORY FOR CORPORATE-STAKEHOLDER RELATIONS

In the context of a systems-based theory of the corporation, managers are not seen as separate from the stakeholder relationship but part of it. It is understood that simply by observing, a participant changes the dynamics of a relationship. In this sense, stakeholder networks cannot be objectified and hence "managed." The multiple human relationships that together constitute social networks are "socially constructed" or co-created.

Therefore, the idea that the corporation is responsible for "managing" stakeholder relationships is not only untenable but counterproductive in the long run for both the corporation and its stakeholders. Stakeholder-management techniques seek to direct and control interactions with stakeholders. Using these techniques, managers often undermine the very relationships they are trying to create.

Formalized contracts with suppliers, for example, ensure compliance but do little to build trust. Issues management, media relations, and external communications, the tools of public affairs specialists, may bring useful information about stakeholder views into the corporation but do little to promote dialogue and ensure that the company's activities are aligned with changing public expectations.

THE IMPORTANCE OF THE EXTERNAL ENVIRONMENT

A systems-based theory of corporate-stakeholder relations leads to new ideas about the responsibilities of corporations, the role of managers, and the most appropriate management style. The formerly influential input-output model led companies to focus on internal functions. Companies re-engineered business processes based on internal analyses irrespective of what was happening in the external environment. These days, when companies must respond quickly to changes in the external environment, an inward focus is not as likely to result in success.

Seeing corporations and their relationship with society from a systems perspective helps us understand that corporations, like organic systems, undergo self-regulation and renewal through interactions with diverse parts of their environment. Healthy companies foster relationships with a variety of stakeholder groups in their external environment. As James Kennelly from the Stern School of Business points out in a recent article, stakeholder networks, like the diverse environments of plants and animals, can be seen as vital pools of participation and diversity that supply organizations with both meaning and valuable resources.[10]

With a strong web of relationships, companies can anticipate, understand, and respond faster and more easily to changes in the external environment. Relationships with external stakeholders, for example, provide companies with invaluable information about external events and market conditions and new technological developments. Information about the external environment is extremely important today because our world is changing so rapidly.

Good relationships with suppliers and other stakeholders can also provide an increased repertoire of insights and responses, greater efficiencies, and more opportunities for creative problem solving. This is especially important because companies must constantly innovate, adapt, and reinvent their products and services to maintain their market share. They must create something new and deliver it in a new way to a new customer base or someone else will.

Finally, strong stakeholder relationships also provide a company with a measure of stability in a turbulent environment. As theorists such as Kennelly and others have argued, businesses, like organisms, can maintain their integrity and core values even amidst chaos, uncertainty, and apparent disintegration. In fact, a company's culture and the stakeholder relationships that govern its behavior help maintain stability in turbulent times.

THE ROLE OF MANAGERS

Agency theory, which has influenced management practice for at least the past fifty years, is based on the premise that managers or *agents* of the owners of a company will tend to be "utility maximizers," acting in an individualistic, opportunistic, and self-serving fashion. This theory is based on a rational, economic model of human beings and reflects some of the basic assumptions that underlie the static "input-output" model of the corporation.

Management theorists are now revising this agency theory of organizations to take into account both the more complex motivations of managers and the influence of social and environmental factors. These emerging ideas about the behavior of managers are based on systems theory.

Peter Block, a writer and consultant known for his classic book *The Empowered Manager*, suggests, for example, that managers can and do operate from a more complex set of values and interests. He uses the term "stewardship," in his book by the same name, to describe a set of beliefs that puts service ahead of self-interest. Employees define themselves as stewards of the organization and beyond that, of the community. Block argues that organizations need to foster a new ethic of stewardship to harness the commitment and energy of their employees and to create an environment that supports change and innovation.

Stewardship offers a new and better framework for understanding how stakeholders can and should influence what corporations do. When managers accept ownership and accountability for the well-being of the larger organization and at the same time give up the need to control others, they are better able to be of service to customers, work in partnership with colleagues and other stakeholders, and develop innovative solutions to problems.

Given the right conditions, managers can and do make choices to support the goals of both the corporation and its stakeholders. They can and do take account of the factors that affect the long-term sustainability of the organization and the community at large.

Within a systems-based theory of the corporation, stewardship makes sense. The primary task of managers is to build and maintain the strong, mutually beneficial stakeholder relationships upon which the corporation depends. This process involves looking for "win-win-win" outcomes at every turn, acting within a sound ethical framework, and balancing the interests of various stakeholders over time to ensure the continued health of the corporation, its stakeholders, and the broader community.

VanCity Credit Union Builds Relationships with Micro Communities: A Case Study

Several years ago, VanCity Credit Union in Vancouver, Canada, embarked upon a program to build relationships with several of its key stakeholders. This is a case study of its "affinity group" program.[11]

VanCity Credit Union is one of the largest credit unions in the world, with over $5 billion in assets. It currently has thirty-two branches located in the Greater Vancouver area. VanCity Credit Union's mission is to be a "democratic, ethical, and innovative provider of financial services to its members. Through strong financial performance, [we] serve as a catalyst for the self-reliance and economic well-being of our membership and the community."

VanCity Credit Union's Statement of Principles

Our Members

We are here to provide members with exceptional service. We aim to offer the best value possible. We are committed to protecting members' assets. We innovate and grow to accompany our members into the future. We provide opportunities for members to promote the economic well-being of their communities.

Our Staff

Staff share in VanCity Credit Union's success because they share its responsibilities. VanCity Credit Union will provide its staff with the resources to deliver exceptional service, with equal opportunities for professional development, and with participation in decision making. VanCity Credit Union is committed to promoting healthy lifestyles for staff and to supporting their personal contributions to the health of the community.

Our Communities

VanCity Credit Union serves as a catalyst for the self-reliance and economic well-being of our membership and the community. Our credit union looks for opportunities to promote the economic development of our community. We support community well-being by funding initiatives that advance positive social change.

Our Ethics

We are honest and fair. We promote the co-operative principles of democracy and participation. We respect each individual. We have social and environmental responsibilities to society. We maintain our integrity by living according to our ethics and we are accountable for our integrity to members and staff.

THE BIRTH OF THE AFFINITY GROUP PROGRAM

In 1989, VanCity Credit Union's Board of Directors identified seven "affinity" groups with whom they wanted to establish closer ties. At VanCity Credit Union, the term "affinity" connotes a sense of joining forces and working together for mutual benefit. The board considered the relative size and profitability potential of each community to the credit union, its historical and natural affiliation with the credit union, the extent to which it was currently underserved by larger financial institutions, and its level of social need.

The affinity-group program was designed to achieve social as well as business goals. VanCity Credit Union's three primary social goals are to promote social justice, to increase economic self-reliance, and to contribute to improving the environment. The original list of affinity groups included ethnic communities (Chinese, East Indian, Italian), churches, gays and lesbians, unions, and women. First Nations were added in 1994.

GETTING STARTED

Between 1990 and 1993, much of the activity centered around raising awareness of VanCity Credit Union within the Italian, East Indian, and Chinese communities. The program began with these three communities because they were large and cohesive.

During this period, VanCity Credit Union's advertising and promotion activities focused on ethnic radio and television and ethnic-language newspapers and magazines. Brochures were produced in several languages, and the credit union sponsored festivals such as the Dragon Boat Festival and the Baisakhi Festival, as well as a popular Italian soap opera that ran weekly on cable television. A separate department at the credit union provided grants to support multicultural and other community initiatives.

At the same time, VanCity Credit Union also hired staff from these communities as part of its corporate-wide diversity program. The organization's policy decision to create a diverse employee group was instrumental in the eventual success of the relationship-building program.

STAFF FOCUS GROUPS PROVIDE DIRECTION

In May 1991, and again in November 1993, focus groups were held to assess marketing initiatives that had been undertaken to that point. Focus groups were held with VanCity Credit Union staff of Italian, Chinese, and East Indian heritage. All credit union staff members were informed of the research and invited to participate if either they or their parents spoke Italian, Hindi, Punjabi, Cantonese, or Mandarin at home and were either immigrants or first- or second-generation descendents of immigrants. Staff members were not paid, but lots of food was provided.

The focus group in 1991 focused on banking habits, criteria for choosing and evaluating financial institutions, awareness of and attitudes toward VanCity Credit Union, communication issues, and preferred media sources. In 1993, the groups focused on awareness of advertising and promotion activities, feedback on in-branch efforts to attract and keep members from the ethnic communities, opportunities to improve the credit union's appeal to the community, and community interests and needs with respect to financial services, as well as broader community services and support.

RESULTS USED TO IMPROVE EARLY MARKETING AND COMMUNITY BUILDING

The focus-group research was instrumental in improving VanCity Credit Union's initial ethnic marketing and community-building efforts. For example, the first set of focus groups revealed that staff members were spending a great deal of time translating brochures for non-English-speaking members. There was clearly a need to provide basic information about VanCity Credit Union products and services and about financial planning in languages other than English.

The research also helped the credit union identify and prioritize community needs for financial services. All three communities tended to be savers as opposed to spenders. Residential mortgages were in demand, though the research also indicated that if VanCity Credit Union was going to tap that market it would have to deal more explicitly with fears about the security of credit unions compared to the "big banks."

Also, it was clear that having staff who spoke these other languages attracted new members from these communities. However, the staff needed to be able to customize products and services. Staff members also reported that to be seen as credible within their community they needed more exposure. To help create exposure and credibility, Italian-speaking staff were profiled in ads prior to the Italian television soap opera. The ideas of focus-group participants were also used to develop or modify certain products and services. For example, multilingual financial planning seminars for those approaching retirement were produced.

INCREASING ORGANIZATIONAL READINESS

The focus groups also helped identify areas where VanCity Credit Union needed to make changes internally before launching into more proactive activities outside the organization. These changes in policies and procedures ensured that the organization was doing as much as it could to support the affinity group community in its regular course of business. Long-term credibility and the effectiveness of the program were at stake. Having staff in the right branches who spoke the language of the customers was key. In addition, all VanCity Credit Union staff needed to be informed about the program, that it was supported by senior management, and that it was an important element of the credit union's long-term strategic plan.

EMPLOYEE TASK GROUPS PROVIDE IDEAS AND OUTREACH

Over the next several years, VanCity Credit Union formed cross-functional internal task groups for each of the affinity groups. Staff from the target communities were invited to participate, and in several instances the groups also included representatives from the community. For example, several Band Chiefs joined the First Nations task group to provide ongoing input.

The task group members contributed cultural knowledge, sensitivity, energy, credibility, and unbounded enthusiasm. They were pleased to be recognized as ambassadors to their community and were excited that they would be able to assist the community and eventually increase the credit union's customer base.

These task groups were responsible for assessing affinity-group activities and developing relationship-building action plans, including budgets. Dr. Boutilier, my business partner, and I supported the formation and development of the task groups and served as a resource to the groups.

RELATIONSHIP BUILDING IN ACTION

Relationship-building efforts increased significantly during this period. The goals in this phase were to assist community-based organizations through employee volunteering and sponsorship of important community events. VanCity Credit Union was also committed to providing needed financial information and advice through community media and seminars.

Task group members and other staff were active in community-based organizations. Some were involved in planning annual cultural festivals, while others were involved in charitable organizations. Through these activities, staff provided the community with skills and knowledge, solidified relationships with community leaders, and established credibility as VanCity Credit Union ambassadors. Some of these activities were conducted during work hours and others were part of the employees' own personal volunteer commitments.

After about six months, task group members developed a list of community events that the credit union could sponsor and made recommendations for media relations and advertising. As active members of the community, they understood the community's needs and identified the media, events, and organizations that would have the greatest visibility and impact. They set sponsorship, partnership, and advertising priorities and gauged the impact of initiatives in terms of awareness-building and business-development potential.

VanCity Credit Union's name became better known during this period, and task group members were successful in bringing new customers to the credit union. Members of the task group also contributed to the identification and assessment of innovative products and services to lure customers from other institutions and to extend and cement relationships with existing customers. Their familiarity with the community made this phase more effective.

DELPHI ASSESSMENT OF AFFINITY-GROUP ACTIVITIES

In early 1996, a qualitative assessment was conducted of all of VanCity Credit Union's affinity group programs with the active participation of task group members and community representatives. Thirty-six staff and board members were involved. A two-stage delphi process[12] was used to allow the status report to be completed in the shortest time possible and to build consensus among those who dealt with affinity groups about what was working, what wasn't, and what future directions should be taken.

In the first round, staff were asked to describe the activities undertaken with their affinity groups and comment on the best approaches and opportunities. For the second round, staff members were provided with summaries of the comments from the others and asked to fill in missing information, to indicate whether they felt the assessments were accurate, and to indicate whether they agreed with the recommendations for future actions.

Beside helping VanCity Credit Union develop better plans for future affinity-group initiatives, the research provided an opportunity to consolidate information about all of the credit union's activities that had a direct impact on the affinity communities and ultimately improved coordination and consistency. As in many large and geographically dispersed organizations, information did not always get communicated from one department to another, and opportunities and problems were not always being addressed.

EXTENSION OF THE PROGRAM

In 1996, VanCity Credit Union decided to more actively pursue relationships with churches and other nonprofit organizations, as well as members of the relatively large gay and lesbian community in Greater Vancouver. The credit union also wanted to assess the feasibility of adding several other ethnic communities to the list of affinity groups. The potential new groups included Korean, Vietnamese, Philippine, Ismaili, and Jewish communities.

Our consulting company was asked to assess the business and relationship-building potential of these seven potential affinity groups. The research was designed to collect information about

- community size and concentration
- values and beliefs
- major community organizations
- important community events and activities
- awareness of and attitudes toward personal finances
- awareness of and attitudes toward VanCity Credit Union and other competitors
- media and communication channels
- promotion opportunities
- opportunities for and barriers to developing business relationships
- recommendations for business and relationship building

The report was based on a review of secondary reports and interviews with over fifty community leaders as well as VanCity Credit Union staff. Interviews with community leaders were beneficial to both the credit union and the community for several reasons. The interviews provided an opportunity to exchange information, to identify common interests, and to build rapport.

The research showed that the credit union's relationship-building efforts were paying off in terms of heightened credibility and positive image. As a result of the affinity-group program, VanCity Credit Union had attracted new members, increased employee morale and loyalty, helped strengthen community organizations, and provided community members with information and tools to become more financially self-sufficient. However, relationship-building efforts were also placing more demands on staff and on budgets that were already stretched. The board was urged to consider the capacity of the organization to take on all seven of the potential new affinity groups.

Prospects for both business development and community development varied across the communities. The nonprofit sector (including but not limited to churches), Philippine-Canadian, and the gay and lesbian communities offered the best balance between social and business opportunities. The Korean, Jewish, and Ismaili communities were relatively affluent and were well served by existing financial institutions. The Vietnamese community had high social action needs but very little business potential in the medium term. The community also lacked cohesiveness and did not have a network of broad-based community organizations that VanCity Credit Union could work with.

The research also indicated that other financial institutions were starting their own niche-marketing campaigns that were threatening VanCity Credit Union's previously unchallenged presence in those communities.

The board approved moving forward with three new affinity groups as recommended. Relationship-building plans were developed for each of the groups to provide the task groups with guidance on media relations and advertising, sponsorship, outreach, and product and service development.

THE VANCITY CREDIT UNION CASE AND THE MODEL OF CORPORATE-STAKEHOLDER RELATIONS

The affinity-group case study shows how one company built stronger relationships with some of its key stakeholders. VanCity Credit Union's affinity-group program was based on both business and social goals that were clear and well aligned with their corporate values. Focus groups with staff from the stakeholder communities provided early and ongoing insight into the character, interests, and needs of those communities. Research with community leaders extended that understanding.

Through its empowered staff task groups, VanCity Credit Union entered into a dialogue with the community and eventually established an implicit contract with community leaders around what the credit union would contribute (i.e., sponsorships, employee volunteer time, financial planning information, customized products and services) and what they expected to receive (i.e., positive reputation, new members).

The relationships between VanCity Credit Union and the affinity communities produced social capital as trust developed between the task group members and senior management and between task group members and community leaders. Intellectual capital was created as staff members gained a better appreciation of the needs of a growing segment of its membership and were able to use that understanding to improve business processes and products. Finally, financial capital was created as new members joined the credit union.

A Guide to FOSTERing Stakeholder Relationships

The nut and the screw form a perfect combination not because they are different, but because they exactly fit into each other and together can perform a function which neither could perform half or alone or any part of alone.

—Mary Parker Follett, 1940

Today, "doing it alone" is less feasible than in the past. Our society is more complex, we are more interdependent on a local as well as a global level, and governments have fewer resources to spend on solving social problems. As one of the leading collaboration theorists, William Isaacs, says, "Thinking alone is no longer adequate. The problems are too complex, interdependencies too intricate, and the consequences of isolation and fragmentation too devastating."[1]

This chapter provides a framework or guide for companies that know that doing it alone is not the best strategy for success. It introduces the acronym "FOSTER" to represent each of six steps for building, or FOSTERing, a web of collaborative stakeholder relationships. "F" is for establishing a solid foundation for relationship building, "O" is for organizational alignment, "S" is for strategy development, "T" is for the process of building trust, "E" is for evaluation, and "R" is for repeat, recognizing that the process of relationship building is continuous. The word "FOSTER" is chosen deliberately as it means "to nourish, to bring up with care and to help grow or develop."[2] The six steps to FOSTERing stakeholder relationships are summarized in table 3.

The chapter begins with a discussion of the meaning and intent of collaboration. Definitions and assumptions are presented next. The FOSTERing guide is introduced by comparing the stages involved in building stakeholder relationships with the stages we all go through in establishing satisfying and mutually beneficial relationships with our friends, family members, and mates. From "playing the field" to "marriage and commitment," the guide provides an easy-to-use framework for companies that want to build and maintain positive stakeholder relationships.

Finding the "Third Way"

"Collaboration is a meta-capability that lies at the heart of new forms of competitive advantage," says Jeanne Liedtka in a recent article in the *Academy of Management Executive Journal*.[3] She argues that the capacity to establish and maintain collaborative relationships, like learning, allows a company to tap into a powerful source of creative energy, a larger pool of innovative ideas, and a broader network.

In some circles, collaboration has a negative connotation. The term "collaborator" was used after the Second World War to describe individuals who colluded with the enemy. Today, however, collaboration has a more positive meaning as a form of partnership that brings individuals from disparate groups together to solve problems or take advantage of mutually beneficial opportunities.

At its best, collaboration enables a meeting of the minds, a collective strategy for problem solving. It has been defined as "a process through which parties who see different aspects of a problem can constructively explore their differences and search for solutions that go beyond their own limited vision of what is possible."[4] True collaboration always involves sharing information, coming up with a common definition of a problem or opportunity, committing to work together, and suspending preconceptions to find and implement new solutions.

Collaboration allows groups to find creative solutions to complex problems. It does not involve unnecessary compromise or domination of some members of the group by others; it offers a means for individuals to get beyond either/or situations to identify "win-win" solutions.

Collaboration clears the road to a "third way," a creative solution based on a synthesis and integration of ideas and information. This notion springs from the writings of Mary P. Follett, whose collected works have recently been republished by the Harvard Business School Press. As she wrote more than fifty years ago, "Integration always involves invention . . . and the clever thing is to recognize this and not to let one's thinking stay within boundaries of two alternatives which are mutually exclusive. In other words, never let yourself be bullied by an either-or situation. . . . find a third way."[5]

Definitions and Scope

POTENTIAL PROBLEMS WITH COLLABORATION

Organizations that develop committed, long-term relationships identify and benefit from win-win solutions and opportunities. However, before embarking on a relationship-building initiative, it is important for organizations to be aware of some of the potential problems and pitfalls.

Collaboration can be costly in human and financial terms. Developing and responding to multiple relationships takes time. Some companies that take on the challenge of creating a more relationship-focused organization may quickly discover that managers lack essential relationship-building skills. Building alliances means sharing control—an anathema to most executives who are used to giving orders and controlling access to information to protect their company's competitive advantage. Giving up control and loosening the reins of authority, depending more on influence than power, is especially difficult when external stakeholder groups such as suppliers and communities are involved.

Also, new or more advanced systems may be required to support collaboration, and communication costs may increase, especially in the short term. In addition, a bid to work cooperatively with another organization may end in failure, precipitating a fracture between the two organizations.

Because stakeholders have different interests or stakes, a single corporate decision may have a positive impact on one stakeholder group while creating hardship for another. A decision may be beneficial for a stakeholder at one time but cause problems for that same group several years later. This situation can lead to conflicts within the organization as the demands and interests of one stakeholder group conflict with the interests of another.

Taking the time to analyze company needs, the strengths and weaknesses of potential partners, and the value and culture fit between a company and various stakeholder organizations will help to ensure that collaborative partnerships are successful.

A CONTINUUM OF COLLABORATIVE RELATIONSHIPS

Collaborative stakeholder relationships exist on a continuum. At one end of the continuum are relationships that involve limited interaction and a narrow scope of joint activity. Companies that consult with stakeholder organizations to foster a greater understanding of each other's goals, interests, and needs would be an example of the "low integration" type of collaborative relationship.

At the "high integration" end, a relationship between a company and its community stakeholders might involve an intensive employee volunteerism program with secondment of executives over several years. A representative from the community might also be invited to sit on the company's board of directors. Similarly, for business-to-business collaboration, the low end might involve joint marketing or distribution of products. At the other end of the continuum are relationships where two or more organizations develop and implement joint business ventures, perhaps sharing staff and resources.

COLLABORATIVE RELATIONSHIPS INVOLVE CYCLICAL PROCESSES OF CHANGE

The process of relationship building is dynamic. Governance structures, membership, the group's focus, and levels of trust evolve and dissolve with time. While the guide identifies several stages of activity, it assumes that relationships are continually shaped and restructured as a result of the actions of collaborative partners.

TRUST BUILDING IS NECESSARY FOR INNOVATION AND COMMITMENT

Most often, collaborative partnerships begin with a small joint activity that involves relatively little risk and requires low levels of trust. Participants learn about their partners and their own needs through these initiatives. Gradually, as trust and mutual understanding develop, the group takes on riskier, more challenging projects. This trust-building process is gradual and incremental.

ESTABLISHING COLLABORATIVE MIND IS ESSENTIAL FOR INNOVATION

A fundamentally important shift from the perspective of innovation and commitment occurs when partners begin to identify with each other and with the group as an "entity." At this point the "collaborative mind" is established and the resulting shared values, language, and stable structure allow a deepening of the relationship, a significant increase in commitment, and a leap forward in terms of capacity for innovation.

Six Stages in FOSTERing Collaborative Relationships

When a company builds collaborative relationships with stakeholders, it is much like the process individuals go through to develop lasting interpersonal relationships. Enduring relationships are based on a foundation of common values and history—the sense of "we." In successful marriages or friendships, the partners are interdependent but also define their boundaries so that while each benefits from the success of the other, each also retains his or her own identity. Partners in successful relationships also learn how to deal with conflict, resolve power struggles, and come to some agreement about behavior with the in-laws or mutual friends. The same is true with building long-term corporate-stakeholder relationships.

In the next section, I introduce a six-step guide to building collaborative stakeholder relationships. Given the growing importance of alliances and the limited amount of time that is available for such initiatives, companies must ensure that their efforts are as efficient and effective as possible. By making the steps involved in building relationships more apparent and the potential pitfalls and opportunities involved in this process more defined, organizations can achieve greater success. A fuller explanation of the steps involved, processes used, and results of each stage is contained in the remaining chapters of the book.

Because of the cyclical and evolving nature of developing relationships, the length and significance of the stages will depend on the complexity of the issues, the type of collaborative venture, and the preexisting level of understanding between the parties.

Each stage, however, involves a number of tasks, the use of various collaboration tools and processes, and a number of outcomes or results. The following table provides a summary of the stages involved in building

Table 3.
A Guide to Building Collaborative Stakeholder Relationships

Stage	Tasks	Tools/Method	Results
Creating a Foundation	• assess relationship building (RB) as a strategic direction • review and refine social mission, values, and ethics • communicate corporate commitment	• strategic planning session with senior management • employee involvement process • dialogue sessions with staff	• decision made to proceed with RB strategy • RB Strategy Group formed • mission, values, and ethical guidelines reviewed and updated • employees aware and supportive
Organizational Alignment	• assess organizational readiness • identify gaps and inconsistencies • assess systems and structures • make changes as needed	• employee survey • systems review • participative processes to facilitate change	• employee mind-sets and skill-sets assessed • systems improved to facilitate relationship building • liabilities resolved
Strategy Development	• inventory and assess existing relationships • benchmark best practices • meet with stakeholders • refine goals and prepare strategy • set up internal structures • begin action planning	• inventory questionnaire • RB Strategy Group workshop • environmental scan • informal dialogue with stakeholders • stakeholder team meetings	• status report on current relationships completed • "best practices" established • priorities identified • views and needs of potential partners understood • goals clarified • stakeholder teams formed • strategy and action plans put in place
Trust building	• exchange information • clarify expectations and perspectives • identify common goals • develop organizational structures • clarify roles and responsibilities, short-term objectives, and timelines • develop and implement "first projects" • identify and resolve areas of conflict • ensure availability of resources	• face-to-face meetings • on-line information system, e-mail • facilitated workshops • experiential events • dialogue • conflict resolution	• access to larger pool of information • increased trust • shared language and vision • more integrated relationships between organizations • innovative solutions • enhanced reputation for both organizations with successful projects
Evaluation	• design and conduct stakeholder audit • celebrate successes • learn from failures	• stakeholder audit • internal dialogue • recognition and reward	• impact of relationship building on corporation measured • regular communication channel with stakeholders established • values aligned between stakeholders and the corporation
Repeat	• repeat steps and refine approach	• RB Strategy Group workshop • consultation with members of stakeholders teams	• relationships continuously improved

collaborative stakeholder relationships and the associated tasks, tools, and anticipated results.

CREATING A FOUNDATION: SOCIAL MISSION, VALUES, AND ETHICAL PRINCIPLES

As most of us who have experienced a failed relationship know, dealing with our own issues, clarifying what we think is important in life as well as our values and our ethical beliefs, is a necessary prerequisite for building strong relationships with others. If we are dishonest, self-centered, or motivated by greed or jealousy, our relationships tend not to be long-lasting. If we have not clarified our needs, we end up in relationships that are unsatisfying and not aligned with our life goals. The same is true of relationships between a company and its stakeholders.

Companies must decide what they stand for, what they want from their stakeholder relationships, and what they expect to get back. They must also develop and operate from a set of values and ethical principles that supports the growth of mutually beneficial relationships. A company's social mission, values, and ethical principles provides employees with a solid foundation for improving existing relationships and for creating new, mutually beneficial stakeholder relationships.

ORGANIZATIONAL ALIGNMENT

Like all imperfect human beings, no organization can ever hope to reach a state of complete readiness for relationship building. Often it is through the process of learning and growth with our partners that we build strengths and overcome our weaknesses.

Nevertheless, assessing and reaching a certain level of organizational readiness will make success more likely. This process involves aligning internal systems and structures to remove barriers and add or strengthen incentives and support mechanisms. The alignment begins with a review of existing systems to identify areas where changes are needed.

Essential systems to support collaboration include rewards and recognition, information systems to promote and support group dialogue, 360-degree communication to foster cross-functional, multilevel internal partnerships, and training and mentoring to ensure staff members have the necessary attitudes and skills. Also needed are structures for participative decision making so that employees can take responsibility for their roles in relationship building and can respond quickly to the opportunities and needs of stakeholder partners.

STRATEGY DEVELOPMENT

To identify strategically important stakeholder partners, companies must first inventory and assess their organization's network of stakeholder relationships. Following the inventory, an environmental scan helps to define gaps and identify future needs. Information is collected about potential stakeholder partners to assess compatibility and to narrow down the list to those with similar values and organizational cultures. With this "short list" in hand, a strategy or action plan can be developed for fostering relationships with these potential partner organizations.

TRUST BUILDING

It is the time-consuming process of building trust that allows collaborative partnerships to survive the inevitable ups and downs that occur in the course of any relationship. Creating and sustaining powerful, innovative collaborative relationships is never easy or quick. The first stage in building trust involves exchanging information and developing structures, roles, and responsibilities that work for everyone. Ideally, partners will establish common goals and identify and plan projects so that the values and experiences of all parties are acknowledged and respected.

As the relationship progresses, trust deepens. Expectations and values are clarified, a shared language and vision for the partnership is established, and the "we" of the relationship is formed. If this environment is created, "collaborative mind" develops, along with the potential for developing "third-way" solutions.

Throughout this trust-building process, there are important steps to take and pitfalls to avoid to ensure that the relationship bears fruit. Collaborative groups must learn how to resolve conflicts and how to communicate effectively, especially about sensitive issues like distribution of rewards and the involvement of host organizations, the in-laws in this analogy. As in any relationship, attention must be given to renewing the relationship and sustaining the commitment of the partners through such vital activities as building and maintaining support of the parent organization, evaluating progress, and celebrating success.

EVALUATION

Every once in a while, it is a good idea to ask our friends or lovers what they think of their relationships with us. Are they happy? Are their needs being met? Are there problems that have been brewing but that have never been talked about or resolved? A regular relationship checkup can often avoid major problems later on. It can also help to open lines of communication and to give each partner a better understanding of the other.

Companies also can benefit from a regular assessment of their relationships. Using a stakeholder audit, companies can

- monitor their performance on key social-relationship goals
- consult with stakeholders to gain an understanding of how they view the company's commitments, the relationship-building process, and the outcome of those relationships
- clarify and improve "social" performance
- build employee and stakeholder support
- increase accountability through the reporting of this information

REPEAT AND IMPROVE RELATIONSHIPS

Relationship building involves ongoing effort and a commitment to continuously learn from, and respond to, the interests and needs of partners. This is why we have included the "repeat" step—there is no end of the road in relationship building.

To nourish relationships and help them grow, companies must regularly seek feedback from their partners and then use that feedback to change their own practices. Evaluation must inevitably lead companies back to the beginning of the process. Are we still committed to this relationship? How can we resolve organizational barriers? What will it take to establish greater levels of trust with our partner?

Corporate Mission, Values, and Ethics—A Foundation for Relationship Building

Truth takes time to be discovered and understood. Trust takes time to be earned. Justice and compassion take time to demonstrate. Mindfulness takes time to practice.

—John Dalla Costa, 1995

Just as shared values, expectations, and trust are the building blocks for successful interpersonal relationships, a company's values, its social mission, and its formal or informal code of ethics serve as an essential foundation for building stakeholder relationships. In this chapter, the focus will be on the first and extremely important stage of building collaborative stakeholder relationships—assessing relationship building as a strategic direction, developing or refining a corporate social mission, clarifying corporate values, fostering an ethical corporate culture, and communicating senior management commitment to stakeholder collaboration.

This chapter will identify the core values that are associated with mutually beneficial collaborative relationships. Case study examples are also used to show how several progressive, collaboration-oriented companies have articulated their social missions and their commitments to their stakeholders.

Relationship Building As a Strategic Direction

The first step in developing a comprehensive relationship-building strategy is to ensure that senior management is committed to the initiative. Given that relationship building takes time and involves some "giving

Table 4.
Creating a Foundation for Relationship Building

Tasks	Tools/Method	Results
• assess relationship building (RB) as a strategic direction	• strategic planning session with senior management	• decision made to proceed with RB strategy
• review and refine social mission, values, and ethics	• employee involvement process	• RB Strategy Group formed
• communicate corporate commitment	• dialogue sessions with staff	• mission, values, and ethical guidelines reviewed and updated
		• employees aware and supportive

before getting," a company's CEO and senior executives must be committed to stakeholder collaboration for it to succeed in the long term. In addition, senior executives must have a long-term view of the bottom-line benefits of relationship building and assume that the company has both an obligation and an interest in helping its stakeholders meet their goals.

Most larger corporations have literally hundreds of stakeholders, and many of these stakeholders interact with different parts of the organization for different purposes at different times. Collaborative partnerships often are not developed for strategic reasons. They may be initiated because the CEO or a member of the senior management team has a personal interest or connection with another company or organization. Or a company may simply react to overtures from stakeholder organizations.

An ad hoc approach to stakeholder relationship building will not necessarily help an organization meet its goals. So it is important that executives reach consensus on whether the company should take on relationship building as part of its overall corporate strategy. Executive involvement is also imperative because the relationship-building initiative will need to be integrated with other corporate strategies and managers may need to advise on the best sequence to use. For example, should the company start by developing more collaborative relationships with other industry partners before launching into relationship building with community partners? Should it establish stronger partnerships with employees before moving outside the organization?

Case Study: Nortel Adopts a Collaborative Approach to Stakeholder Relations

Northern Telecom (Nortel), a North American telecommunications giant, is one of the few companies worldwide that has developed a comprehensive and strategic program for building collaborative stakeholder relationships. In its 1996 "Environment, Health, and Safety Report," the company laid out its commitments to stakeholders and the reasons why it believes these relationships are critical to long-term success.

In the early 1990s, shareholders were the number one priority for Nortel. Customers were also important but less attention was paid to employees, suppliers, and communities. This ordering of stakeholder priorities began to shift in 1994 when the results of an employee opinion survey were matched up with customer surveys, showing a correlation between employee satisfaction and customer satisfaction.

At the same time, Nortel was reviewing its code of conduct and held focus groups with staff to solicit input about the revision of its code. Staff members from all areas of the company were vocal in their recommendations that the company improve relationships with employees, communities, and suppliers and incorporate these goals into the code of conduct.

Because Nortel's environmental management and reporting programs, established in the early 1990s, had paid dividends in terms of cost savings as well as public image, senior managers were willing to consider broader stakeholder needs and interests. While the staff still needed to present a business case for stakeholder relationship building, senior management already understood that such a shift in orientation could have short- and long-term benefits and would be important for ethical as well as managerial reasons.

There were barriers, however. Employees and managers were already under pressure trying to meet demands for quality, timeliness, and innovation. They needed to be convinced that relationship building was worth their time and effort and to see that such efforts would be rewarded in terms of performance reviews. So the committee leading this initiative started an internal communications process to raise awareness and solicit feedback. Concerns were identified and communicated across departments. This communication process was effective, partly because the change processes put in place for the Total Quality Management program instilled in employees the idea that relationship building was everyone's business and that they had some responsibility for its success.

Other difficulties also have yet to be overcome. The company has to develop new measures to assess the impact of stakeholder relationships and to define the companies' own objectives and limitations. Also, while commitments have been made in some parts of the company with respect to the company's impact on the environment and the health and safety of workers, they have not been formally adopted by other divisions of this large company. Extending these commitments to other stakeholders, such as investors and suppliers, will likely present unforeseen challenges and pressures.

The following is Nortel's statement of its commitment to its stakeholders as it appears on the company's web site:

Nortel's Stakeholder Commitments[1]

Customers

Delivering value to customers has always been a priority at Nortel. In the past, we focused primarily on producing high quality, well-priced products. Now, we're broadening our approach. In these fast-moving times, solutions are increasingly complex and customized. That's one reason we're committed to building closer ties with our customers. We need to continue to learn about what they value so we can tailor our goods and services to meet their needs.

Employees

Nortel recognizes the fundamental role that employees play in achieving business success. We're committed to protecting and enhancing the health and well-being of our employees, to providing an environment in which they can work safely and productively— wherever in the world their job takes them—and to treating individuals with respect and dignity. We believe these commitments benefit employees through improved quality of life and job satisfaction. These commitments benefit customers because they contribute to our ability to attract and retain high quality employees, and to create an environment that allows them to perform to the optimum. Ultimately this pays off in improved shareholder value.

Suppliers

Just as we're aiming to build loyal relationships with our customers, we want to develop long-term, mutually beneficial relationships with our key suppliers. Nortel's goal is to create network solutions that provide the highest value, while consuming the minimum amount of materials and energy, and generating the least amount of waste. Our purchasing decisions are based on criteria such as competitive pricing, quality and service, but they're also influenced by the environmental and ethical standards of our suppliers.

Local Communities

Wherever we're located, Nortel is committed to being a model corporate citizen. Our ambitious environmental performance targets are pushing us to minimize the impact of our operations. As a corporation, and through the initiative of individual employees, we're actively contributing to the general well-being of the towns, cities, and regions in which we're working, through the sharing of skills and expertise in areas such as environmental protection, health and safety.

Global Communities

A global corporation faces a special challenge. We need to uphold consistent corporate standards of ethical and socially responsible business conduct, while respecting the culture and business customs of the varying locations in which we operate. Nortel's initiatives take into account the social aims and economic priorities of each country in which we do business, while helping maintain consistently high environmental, health and safety standards.

What Is a Social Mission?

Most companies have developed a mission statement that lays out the primary aims of the organization. For some companies, the mission statement addresses a narrow set of aims, often related to profitability and serving the interests of stockholders. Sometimes an organization's social mission—or its understanding of its responsibilities to its other stakeholders—is unstated or very loosely articulated. Sometimes this mission is simply recognized as "the way things are done."

A social mission statement is an important piece of the foundation for relationship building because it links the company's bottom-line business goals with its broader social goals and responsibilities and defines the balance the company expects to maintain between financial and nonfinancial outcomes. It also reflects the organization's core values. VanCity Credit Union's mission statement is a good example of one that incorporates a broader social context.

> Vancouver City Savings Credit Union is a democratic, ethical and innovative provider of financial services to its members. Through strong financial performance, we serve as a catalyst for the self-reliance and economic well-being of our membership and the community.

DEVELOPING A SOCIAL MISSION

Involving employees in a process of developing and formalizing a social mission can be a useful mechanism for both generating internal understanding and commitment and for clarifying corporate aims and commitments so they are understood by external stakeholders. When employees and management share a vision for the company that goes beyond making money, ideas can be shared and solutions developed efficiently and creatively. With such a common vision, the potential for learning and productivity also increases.

The process of relationship building can evoke a sense of purpose and community that will motivate and inspire employees and create the internal momentum to ensure that the relationship-building goals are met. While involving all employees may not be possible, the following example will give some ideas about what can be done. Glaxo Wellcome, Inc., involved its employees in developing the goals for its community-involvement program within its overall social mission.

Case Study: Glaxo Wellcome's Social Mission

Glaxo Wellcome, a multinational pharmaceutical company, has developed a broad-based social mission statement for its Canadian operations. The statement affirms the company's commitment to making a "positive difference to quality of life" in both the laboratory and the community. It also explicitly defines the company's social values, including a concern with the health and social well-being of communities, the capacity of people to care for one another, the ability of people to manage their health and maintain their independence, and the opportunity to prevent problems before they arise.

The mission statement affirms the company's commitment to develop collaborative and constructive working relationships with outside organizations and indicates that the company will go beyond providing financial support to offering guidance, expertise, in-kind donations, helpful connections, and the volunteer involvement of employees.

In 1996, the Glaxo Wellcome Foundation in Canada decided to make a substantial long-term commitment to a social cause that would strengthen its ties to the community and create stronger bonds among employees. The search for a cause began when the executive committee agreed on the need to develop a coherent social focus for the company's philanthropic activities. A vice president championed the idea and others further down the corporate ladder were interested and supportive.

The social focus was especially important because the company had recently merged with another firm with a distinct corporate culture and its own set of values. The executive committee felt that a social focus would serve as a unifying force, bringing the two cultures closer together.

The executive committee set two criteria for a social focus: it should be integrated with Glaxo Wellcome's business interests and employees should be involved in identifying and carrying out the initiatives.

A small cross-functional team was formed to design and coordinate the project. As a first step, an employee survey determined which areas of community involvement were most widely supported. Forty-two percent of Glaxo Wellcome's 1,200 employees responded to the survey. Almost all felt that the company should be giving something back to the community, and health was their number one concern.

A committee of employees from all levels of the company except the executive suite assessed causes that reflected their co-workers' concerns with health and the community. This assessment spanned several months and included a two-day retreat.

At the retreat, the group discussed individual and corporate values and issues such as commitment. The group identified criteria for selecting a social cause, drew up a long list of sixty ideas for involvement, and then reduced it to a short list of four "cause communities."

The group then consulted with external representatives from the four cause communities to determine the level and type of community need and the fit of each cause with corporate objectives.

A strong internal communications program encouraged and supported employee discussions and debate. Brown-bag lunches, brochures, tent cards in the employee cafeteria, and articles in the company newsletter provided information about the pros and cons of the four causes.

In January 1997, the employees voted on their preferred charitable cause. They chose hospice care, a holistic form of care that improves the quality of life for terminally ill people and their families.

Glaxo Wellcome has begun a collaborative process with hospice organizations across Canada to determine how the company and its employees can support the hospice movement. One possible area of involvement is helping hospice organizations share information resources, develop policy, and increase public awareness on a national level. Already this project is receiving positive attention from the media and support from other organizations.

Corporate Values That Support Collaboration

Corporate values, whether explicitly stated and formalized or implicit and informal, influence day-to-day practices as well as stakeholder-specific goals and strategies. Some values such as stewardship or mutuality are cornerstones for a collaborative organization. An organization's corporate culture and the values it embodies can support or discourage productive collaboration. Corporate values will define how relationships are developed and, to a large extent, whether or not they are successful.

Corporations have a variety of important stakeholders, and in some cases, the interests and demands of those stakeholders can conflict with one another. Establishing a corporate culture based on a set of sound values and principles will provide the context within which ethical and just decisions can be made—decisions that support the long-term interests of the organization and the stability of its relationships.

As Mary Follett wrote over fifty years ago, "Business should realize that it is responsible to something higher than the public will of a community, that its service to the public does not lie wholly in obeying the public." A strong set of corporate values will help firms define the "something higher" to which she refers.

Following are some of the values that are most essential for companies engaged in strengthening collaborative relationships. Consider to what extent your organization embodies these values and beliefs.

SYSTEMS THINKING

Systems thinking is central to collaboration in that it places the organization within the web of relationships that define and sustain it. A systems view of the world implies a focus on the whole, not just the constituent parts. To identify and establish productive relationships, an organization and its employees must understand how they fit into the larger systems of which they are a part.

Systems thinking also assumes that individuals are actively involved in constructing reality, in interpreting information, and in making meaning for themselves and with others.[2] From a systems perspective, managers and employees are seen as playing an active part in constructing relationships with stakeholders. Systems theory also recognizes the dynamic nature of those relationships and the importance of creating a shared understanding of each other's assumptions and beliefs.

STEWARDSHIP/SERVICE

Stewardship involves a set of beliefs that puts service over the pursuit of self-interest. Within this set of values and beliefs, employees, for example, see themselves as stewards of the organization and, beyond that, the community. Individuals who see themselves as stewards are naturally committed to ensuring the well-being of others and the sustainability of the enterprise and the broader society.

Stewardship is also aligned with the notion of reciprocity, the idea that give and take are necessary and desirable sides to every relationship—

even in business. Reciprocity is fundamental to building collaborative relationships with stakeholders.

AUTHENTICITY AND TRUST

For relationships to thrive, all partners must have a sense that the other parties have their best interests at heart and that they will act honorably and fairly. Studies show that ethical behavior is a precursor of trust, and trust is essential for building strong relationships with customers, suppliers, employees, and the public.

Communicating ideas honestly and respectfully is essential for creating trust and the conditions necessary for collaboration. Sharing ideas in a collaborative relationship means that people are vulnerable and are exposed to ambiguity and conflict. People need to trust each other to take these risks and to allow sharing to occur.

Organizations that encourage authentic, honest, and respectful dialogue create an environment where disagreements and conflict become a valuable source of learning. When individuals can communicate their thoughts and feelings honestly and without fear, the creativity and productivity of collaborative ventures increases exponentially.

WISDOM OF THE INDIVIDUAL

Everyone has a contribution to make. Each of us has inner wisdom and holds a part of the truth. This belief is key to establishing productive relationships with stakeholders. It broadens leadership and results in more decentralized decision making within the organization and more egalitarian relationships between staff at different levels. Employees who believe in the wisdom of the individual will believe that external stakeholders have an important and meaningful contribution to make.

SPIRIT OF INQUIRY/RISK TAKING/EXPERIMENTATION

Companies that encourage their employees to take risks and to learn from situations and experiences will be more likely to benefit from stakeholder relationships. Staff involved in building relationships inside and outside the organization will be more likely to identify opportunities, develop innovative solutions, and continuously adapt to changing realities if the corporate culture is dynamic and supports experimentation.

Creating an Ethical Corporate Culture

PROBLEMS WITH ETHICAL CODES AND GUIDELINES

Unethical behavior can cost companies hefty fines, a tarnished public reputation, and eroded trust in stakeholder relationships. Texaco, Inc., recently had to pay $176 million when taped evidence of executive-level discrimination was used in a lawsuit. Bausch & Lomb Inc.'s earnings fell 54 percent several years ago when managers' behavior and accounting practices were found to be unethical.[3]

In 1991, U.S. federal sentencing guidelines were changed so that companies without mechanisms to prevent and detect ethics violations would receive higher fines than those who did. Companies were being encouraged with the threat of fines to identify and put a halt to poor management practices, racial and gender discrimination, quality and safety defects, environmental pollution, and the use of inaccurate and false records.[4]

Many American companies responded by developing codes of ethics that were framed, mounted, and quickly forgotten. According to a recent study in *California Management Review,* corporate ethics programs, codes of conduct, mission statements, and hot lines make little difference to employees.[5] This is because they fail to address issues faced by young managers, are not tied to the reward system, and are not consistent with actual corporate behavior.

A recent study of ethics codes at 175 companies, conducted by the Centre for Corporate Social Performance and Ethics at the University of Toronto Faculty of Management, identified a number of additional problems with traditional codes of ethics:[6]

- In-house lawyers are often asked to prepare codes of ethics. The resulting emphasis on legalistic parameters doesn't foster compliance or generate support among employees.

- Codes tend to be too corporation-centered and don't take account of the perspectives and needs of other stakeholders such as suppliers, customers, and communities.

- Codes developed in one country are not necessarily applicable in another because of local cultures and traditions.

- Senior managers don't always visibly demonstrate their support for the code through their behavior.

HOW TO DEVELOP AN ETHICAL CULTURE

As expected, simply creating a code of ethics does not improve ethical behavior or minimize violations. Nor does a code of ethics necessarily contribute to the development of strong, trust-based, mutually beneficial relationships. In a stakeholder-oriented company, ethical behavior cannot be prescribed, commanded, or controlled. A code of conduct that specifies what an employee must or must not do in every circumstance is not only impractical, but it would be inconsistent with a more democratic, egalitarian culture. Even a code of practice that defines "how things are usually done" is difficult to establish in a stakeholder-oriented company because relationships are constantly changing and evolving.

What can be done? Some initiatives are broad in scope. They involve creating the conditions that allow individuals to contribute all that they can: supporting the ability of employees to self-organize, recognizing the talents and skills of each individual, and supporting the employees as they change and grow.

Besides valuing the contributions of each individual, creating an ethical corporate culture also involves creating the freedom for individuals to act. As well-known writer Elizabeth Pinchot said in an article called "Can We Afford Ethics?" "Human self-organizing systems depend on the units within the systems to behave even when they are not watched, even when there are no penalties for misbehavior. For higher levels of interconnection to manifest, there must be trust, and that trust must be based on an assurance of the goodness of others in the system."[7]

Process is also important. Employees should be actively engaged in shaping and refining the corporate social mission, values, and ethical guidelines so that the personal values of most employees and those of the corporation are aligned. Social psychologists have found intrinsic (internal) motivation produces longer-lasting behavior changes than extrinsic motivation, which can produce initial compliance, followed by attempts to subvert the rules, and a return to old behaviors once the rules change or the incentives disappear.

Also, employees should have the decision-making skills, knowledge, and competencies needed to make ethically sound decisions on a day-to-day basis. This means companies must raise awareness so that employees recognize ethical problems, provide the training and support so that when employees spot an ethical problem they are able to think it through, and finally, put the necessary structures in place to allow employees to take action if an ethical problem arises and allow the company to monitor and respond if unethical behavior occurs.

BASIC ETHICAL PRINCIPLES

The substance of a company's guidelines for ethical behavior should reflect the corporation's social mission and goals and its values. A number of moral or ethical principles are common around the world. Rushworth Kidder, founder of the Institute for Global Ethics, suggests that there are at least five universal ethical principles:

1. *Respect for human dignity:* never to demean another person, to be respectful, to ensure everyone has common rights

2. *Freedom:* to be free of violence and stealing, to be able to determine our actions without fear of subjugation

3. *Compassion:* to act from love, to support one another

4. *Tolerance for diversity:* the right to differ with authority

5. *The Golden Rule:* to treat others the way we'd like to be treated[8]

Dialogue sessions (see chapter 6 for a description of this process) with small groups can be used to develop guidelines for ethical behavior and standards appropriate for the organization and its employees. Sustained efforts are needed, however, to ensure that all employees internalize corporate commitments and values and that monitoring and compliance mechanisms are effective.

Communicating Corporate Commitment and Values

For a company to move toward collaboration, corporate values and commitments to stakeholders should be clearly and frequently communicated. Company leaders should be personally committed, credible, and willing to "walk the talk" of corporate values and commitments. These values should be integrated into decision-making processes and reflected in the organization's critical activities.

The following are some possible communications tools and strategies:

- Set up CEO-employee meetings to discuss the benefits and rationale for stakeholder collaboration (brown bag lunches, question and answer sessions).

- Create opportunities for informal conversations between senior management and employees (organize office space and lunchrooms to facilitate informal communication, encourage senior managers to visit the "shop floor").

- Encourage storytelling (CEO talks about benefits of collaboration in speeches or newsletter articles).

- Identify examples of positive internal or external collaboration and publicize positive results.

- Ask staff who are already involved in relationship building to share information and solicit feedback from other employees.

Aligning Corporate Systems and Structures

Organization(s) must cultivate equity, autonomy and individual opportunity. . . . The governing structure must not be a chain of command, but rather a framework for dialogue, deliberation and coordination among equals.

—Dee Hock, 1996

This chapter will focus on the process of aligning internal systems and structures to support collaboration. First it will explain why it is important to align internal systems before reaching outside the organization to build relationships. Then it will describe the systems and structures that are most critical to collaboration—from participative management systems to communication, rewards, and information systems—as well as look briefly at the changes in mind-sets and skill-sets that are required for collaboration to become widely practiced within an organization. A case study is presented to show how both individual and structural barriers within one organization prevented it from building positive relationships with external stakeholders.

Next, the chapter will describe the process of assessing an organization's readiness for collaboration. The assessment process includes an employee survey to determine awareness of and attitudes toward collaboration and a review of existing policies, programs, and management systems to identify gaps, inconsistencies, and strengths.

Finally, the chapter will briefly introduce some organizational-change methods that are particularly suited to helping organizations become more collaborative.

Table 5.
Organizational Alignment

Tasks	Tools/Method	Results
• assess organizational readiness	• employee survey	• employee mind-sets and skill-sets assessed
• identify gaps and inconsistencies	• systems review	• systems improved to facilitate relationship building
• assess systems and structures	• participative processes to facilitate change	• liabilities resolved
• make changes as needed		

Why Align Systems Before Reaching Out to Build Relationships?

Creating internal structures and systems that support collaboration will help to ensure effective relationship building. A great deal of time and resources can be wasted, despite the best intentions of skilled employees, if an organization's system and structures discourage collaboration by, for instance, limiting communication, creating unnecessary time delays, or making it difficult to obtain the resources needed for new partnership development.

Ensuring that individual staff members who are involved in relationship building have the motivation and skills to identify partnership opportunities and to communicate and negotiate effectively with others can also substantially increase the impact of relationship building initiatives outside the organization. It is important to identify the overall level of awareness and understanding of key issues as well as the skill level and motivation held by individual employees.

Collaboration skills are also important for internal collaboration. For example, a cross-functional team with representatives from community relations, marketing, human resources, and operations could play a pivotal role in planning and implementing an employee volunteer program. Staff from the sales, product development, finance, and marketing departments may need to collaborate in order to plan and carry out a joint-venture development project with a supplier. Employees, just like organizations, can be at various places along the continuum of readiness for collaboration.

Systems and Structures That Support Collaboration

BOUNDARYLESS ORGANIZATIONS DEPEND ON COLLABORATION

Stakeholder collaboration is a fundamental characteristic of more organic, boundaryless organizations. As the authors of the best selling book *The Boundaryless Organization*[1] point out, to be successful in a highly competitive, turbulent environment, companies need to have more permeable and fluid boundaries to allow information, ideas, and people to be moved quickly and efficiently to where they are needed. Boundaryless organizations depend on collaboration.

Information and ideas are sought from all levels of the organization, from within departments, and from external stakeholders, including customers, suppliers, communities, government agencies, and others from around the world. Important problems or new opportunities are tackled by teams with members from throughout the organization. Customers and suppliers contribute to new product and process ideas and also are able to access the resources, including the time and advice of senior managers, of the corporations they do business with.

HIGH-INVOLVEMENT ORGANIZATIONS FOSTER COLLABORATION

High-involvement organizations create the conditions within which collaborative relationships flourish. What does a high-involvement organization look like? First, senior executives communicate and reinforce the corporation's commitment to collaboration and the importance of values such as reciprocity, authenticity, and trust.

Second, open and truthful communication is encouraged, red tape is removed, and cross-functional teams are part of everyday work life. These teams, with members from different levels and parts of the organization, identify and mobilize project-related resources and maintain communication within the organization. Decision-making authority is put in the hands of people most closely linked to the work involved.

Third, employees contribute ideas to increase corporate effectiveness and share in the profits of the company. They develop a spirit of cooperation and gain the skills necessary to establish and maintain positive relationships with others.

High-involvement organizations emphasize the just and equitable treatment of all employees, thus building trust—one of the essential conditions for relationship building. When workers identify with organizational goals and values and are intrinsically motivated by those goals, they are more likely to focus on cooperation and collaboration rather than their own personal agendas.[2] There is a direct correlation between how employees are treated and how they treat customers, suppliers, and other strategic partners.

RESEARCH LINKS ORGANIZATIONAL SYSTEMS WITH THE CAPACITY FOR RELATIONSHIP BUILDING

Several empirical studies illustrate the link between internal organizational systems, structures, and management philosophies and the capacity of a company to build collaborative relationships with internal and external stakeholders. A study of seven insurance companies, for example, found that companies with a collaborative approach to problem solving and a stakeholder-oriented management philosophy were rated most positively by external stakeholders based on a long list of social performance measures. Those that were rated as the worst had a more adversarial management philosophy in which short-term, bottom-line concerns took precedence over other, longer-term considerations.[3]

Another recent study looked at the impact of changes in management and decision-making structures and processes on the quality of external stakeholder relationships.[4] The study looked at four companies that had institutionalized gainsharing (profit sharing), and the involvement of nonmanagement employees in problem-solving and decision-making teams. These changes led to a number of positive outcomes including benefits for the company's owners in terms of cost savings, its customers in terms of improved product quality and service, its suppliers in terms of feedback on their products, and its production employees in terms of improved health and safety conditions. A more collaborative internal management structure had a strong positive impact on the company's relations with employees, owners, customers, suppliers, and even the natural environment.

The researchers noted that shortly after the internal changes were made a sense of partnership quickly developed between management and nonmanagement employees. At one company, this new partnership resulted in nonmanagement employees seeking higher quality products from suppliers, causing management to rethink its previous adversarial relationship with suppliers. Suppliers were invited to meet with production employees to identify ways to improve their products. At another company, employees addressed the problems of energy inefficiency, excessive scrap, and product wastes shortly after the profit-sharing plan was introduced. An office worker used the newly implemented suggestion system to gain support for a paper-recycling program that had previously been discounted by management. As the program started to save the company money, management became more supportive of other environmental initiatives.

Internal and External Communication Systems

In addition to a participative, high-involvement management style and structure, effective collaboration depends on multiway communication. As Frank Sonnenberg writes in his book *Managing with a Conscience*, "Employees must feel free to network with anyone who has the necessary information to accomplish an activity, without regard to level, business unit, or other artificial boundary."[5] This formal and informal communication takes place among

- employees within the organization
- employees and the organization's leadership
- the organization and its external partners

Encouraging lateral and diagonal communications between all levels of the organization and across divisional boundaries helps to avoid duplication of effort and inconsistencies in the way corporate values and the social mission are expressed. The ability of cross-functional teams to operate effectively depends on their ability to integrate departmental goals, to learn each other's specialized language, and to develop a sense of unity.

Intensive communication by senior management reinforces the value of collaboration. Also, if the social mission was developed with input from all employees, it should connect with each employee's personal values and sense of responsibility for the organization and its stakeholders. When this integration exists and the social mission is reinforced continually by senior management, employees will adopt it as their own and it will be communicated continuously to customers, suppliers, friends, and neighbors.

Corporate commitment to collaboration can also be communicated through rituals and physical means, such as the design of meeting rooms. Employee forums can encourage people to get to know one another. Informal "living room" meeting spaces that are accessible and inviting to all can foster informal conversations.

Recently, Nortel received an award from *Business Week/Architectural Record* for its employee-designed office headquarters. The new facilities included a garden, health/wellness center, bank, travel agency, and work areas for visiting employees. According to Nortel, the new workspace has facilitated teamwork, increased creativity, and led to a spirit of innovation. Nortel says it has recovered all of the renovation costs and saved over $225 million.[6]

Information Systems

For collaboration to work inside or outside the organization, employees need to be able to share information, coordinate their actions, and engage in dialogue as a means to generate new ideas. The effectiveness of these activities can be increased dramatically with new technology. As management theorist John Henderson says, "We must change how long it takes us to think strategically. To do that, we need the technology that enables us to examine the competitive environment, think about it effectively, and come to some decisions. That kind of partnership requires significant information technology support."[7]

Relationship building also requires that a company serve its customers' needs seamlessly. One of the key ingredients in seamless service delivery is a computer system that permits information sharing across departments and functional areas. The role of technology in supporting the move to relationship building cannot be overstated. The lack of computer systems that allow for tracking of information about each customer's needs is often the greatest barrier to building customer relationships.

The following is a brief review of the kinds of information systems that are available to support collaborative relationship building.

SYSTEMS TO SHARE INFORMATION

Building relationships among team members within an organization requires equal access to good information. Cross-functional teams that are engaged in creating alliances with external organizations need to be able to share information. Information sharing among individuals who may not be physically close to one another can be supported by establishing databases of ideas and core documents. Individual participants can access these documents and over time develop a common frame of reference and set of ideas. The Internet can provide essential support to the development of collaborative relationships.

Hypermedia systems (the World Wide Web, for example) allow individuals to create, annotate, link together, and share information from a variety of media including text, graphics, audio, video, and images.[8] Finally, simple mechanisms such as bulletin boards for posting news or electronic lists of employees that document their areas of expertise, current projects, and interests can also facilitate cross fertilization of ideas and support collaborative ventures.

Case Study: Networking and Information Sharing at Wal-Mart

Wal-Mart Stores, Inc., one of the United States' largest and most profitable retailers, places a great deal of importance on supporting formal and informal networking and information sharing among managers, suppliers, and customers. According to industry experts, Wal-Mart's success has hinged on its ability to understand and satisfy customer needs through innovative business processes, many of which depend on collaboration between employees and suppliers.[9]

For example, cross-docking, one of Wal-Mart's most innovative business processes, involves receiving and repackaging goods at warehouses. Goods are then quickly moved to another "dock" for shipment to stores, usually within 48 hours. Cross-docking requires intensive coordination and collaboration between employees and suppliers as well as use of real-time information received by satellite to ensure that orders can flow in and be consolidated and executed within a matter of hours. Wal-Mart staff members are able to achieve short turnaround times so that stock can be replenished quickly. The result is increased customer satisfaction and higher profits.

Since its store managers have considerable autonomy, Wal-Mart ensures that they learn from each other and from the marketplace. It has instituted procedures to gather information about consumers and its competition so that managers can use it to develop innovative responses. That process is referred to as "quick market intelligence" (QMI).

Each week two hundred or more Wal-Mart senior executives and managers visit stores and competitors across the country to see what is selling and what isn't. They talk to customers and managers. After three days, they "huddle" with their counterparts in a full-day meeting to analyze quantitative data about sales and to share their impressions. Then they make decisions about products and promotions and share the results by teleconference with over 1,800 stores.

Wal-Mart also builds close relationships with its suppliers, and although it expects them to adapt to its delivery systems and offer their products at low prices, it pays more quickly and does not change suppliers very often, in order to get the lowest price.

Wal-Mart's competitive advantage appears to be linked more to how it operates than to where it is located and what it sells. Its success stems from its ability to anticipate trends, maintain flexibility, and foster effective decentralized decision making through collaborative processes.

SYSTEMS TO ENCOURAGE CONVERSATIONS

Information systems can also be used to support the joint construction and dissemination of experiences and insights. Senior staff members can be "on call" through their telephones, fax machines, or e-mail to talk about and advise on new projects. Groups of employees can form informal "communities of practice"[10] to share information and engage in ongoing conversations.

"Groupware" is any type of multiuser software that enables people to participate in the on-line creation and editing of documents, supports feedback and review among team members, and assists discussions. The term was coined in the late 1970s by Trudy and Peter Johnson-Lenz.

Participants use keypads to indicate individual opinions or preferences while the computer graphically displays the whole group's responses.

Electronic meeting systems allow participants on networked computers to be led by a facilitator through a process of generating and evaluating new ideas.[11] Similarly, multimedia communications allow groups to create graphic models, clarify processes, and integrate actions and activities. Group calendars and workflow management systems can help ensure timely participation of members.

SYSTEMS TO IMPROVE COORDINATION

Joint action or collaborative ventures often require that individuals understand each other's work environment, including technology and business practices. Developing this understanding is aided by the use of multimedia conference systems to simulate face-to-face meetings across time zones. Live video transmission, joint authoring of documents, and on-line discussions also help groups coordinate their activities.

Some of these systems can preserve the anonymity of participants so members can openly discuss controversial ideas or issues. This can lead to greater interaction, equal participation, objectivity, and better problem solving.

Tools to support organizational memory also can help to ensure continuity and consistency when membership in a group changes often.[12] Hard data (numbers, facts, figures, rules, etc.) as well as soft information (tacit knowledge, expertise, experience, anecdotes, critical incidents, stories, details about strategic decisions, etc.) can be accessed using document-management systems such as navigation aids, queries, and personalized pathways.

New Mind-Set, Skill-Set, and Organizational Support

Stakeholder collaboration, which involves two or more people working together to find creative, mutually beneficial solutions, cannot be mandated or legislated. It is an evolving process, and its success depends on the commitment and skills of individual employees as well as on the resources and the formal and informal support provided by a company.

In a recent article in the *Academy of Management Review*, Jeanne Liedtka argues that collaboration requires a partnering mind-set and skill-set and a supportive organizational context.[13] She suggests that managers need to develop a collaborative mind-set to deal with the risks and challenges involved in working across traditional boundaries and to sustain the level of effort that is required to develop relationships when current workplace demands are already high.

She also points out that collaboration and partnership building relies on skills that have not been rewarded in the past including "listening with an open mind to the proposals of others versus selling one's own solution harder; acknowledging and using conflict productively versus suppressing and ignoring it; leading by supporting and facilitating versus managing through authority or fiat."[14]

The following case study illustrates how a combination of employee attitudes and structural barriers prevented one organization from building strong stakeholder relationships.

Case Study: Poor Stakeholder Relationships Stall Corporate Activity

The Housing Development Corporation (HDC)[15] administers and maintains government-owned public housing, assists in the management of rental housing operated by nonprofit organizations, and forms partnerships with nonprofit community organizations to build affordable housing. In 1997, the HDC was embroiled in several high-profile conflicts with citizens who were opposed to the siting of group homes and other public housing complexes in their areas. These conflicts threatened to prevent the HDC from carrying out its mandate to build affordable housing. In order to address the NIMBY ("not in my backyard") problem, the HDC first addressed organizational issues that were contributing to poor community relations and then developed a partnership plan with its key stakeholders to build public support for public housing.

The HDC had already developed a strategic plan for the organization that identified building public support and forging stronger stakeholder relationships as key strategic directions for the following year. They had also developed a clear and widely supported mission statement and set of values. A cross-functional team was set up to coordinate the stakeholder relations project. Our firm was hired to work with the HDC to develop a plan for building the support of neighbors, tenants, and communities and for building relationships with HDC's partners, including architects, developers, nonprofit housing societies, and other community agencies.

As a first step, our firm met one-on-one with twenty-five HDC staff members who represented a cross section of the company to identify important issues and to gather ideas about what needed to be covered in a staff workshop. As outside consultants, we were able to identify sensitive issues that affected the capacity of the whole organization to manage relationships with external partners and communities.

Then forty HDC staff from various departments participated in a full-day workshop to identify the internal systems and structures as well as the values and attitudes that were contributing to the difficulties and conflicts with external stockholders. It turned out that differences in operating styles and perspectives across the three HDC departments had a significant effect on relationships with external stakeholders.

One department was primarily involved in the purchase of the property. Members of this group focused on finding a site and purchasing the property for the lowest price possible. The zeal of property agents to "get the best price" often meant that the purchaser and the intended use of the property was not announced until after the property was purchased. This led to mistrust and frustration on the part of many local residents who felt duped when they found out that a public housing project was going to be built in their neighborhood.

The second group was made up of project officers who were mainly involved in the design and construction process. While familiar with community relations techniques, their focus was on completing projects on time and on budget. The "just get it done" orientation of the project officers did ensure that the projects were finished on time, but often relationships with external partners became strained as a result. Also, the potential for working with them to anticipate and resolve community concerns was not realized.

Members of the third group, management services staff, on the other hand, were primarily involved with managing the projects after they were built. Their focus was on resolving conflicts, coordinating health and other services for low income tenants, and managing relationships. They had been marginalized within the HDC organization and the result was limited use of their relationship-building skills outside the property management stage.

In addition to values and attitudes, other more basic barriers to internal collaboration were identified. Computer systems were not compatible across the three departments, cross-departmental meetings were rarely held, and as a consequence, the staff members did not share information and were not well acquainted with the activities of the other departments. Workshop participants agreed that resolving internal barriers was a necessary first step before developing new community relations and partnership-building strategies. The following table summarizes some of the important barriers and solutions.

Table 6
Summary of Internal Barriers and Solutions

Internal Barriers to Effective Community Relations	Solutions
Unclear and conflicting expectations	Clarify staff roles in dealing with internal and external partners
Hierarchical structure and limited flexibility at the staff level	Establish cross-functional, team-based management
Lack of internal coordination	Integrate computer systems
Cumbersome policies and procedures	Streamline approval process
Delays caused by an emphasis on risk control	Take a more strategic approach to risk assessment and management

Rewards and Recognition

The transition to a more collaborative corporate culture requires more than good communication and information systems. Employees must not only understand and adopt the social mission and collaborative values as their own, but they must be rewarded and recognized for doing so. In general, reward and recognition systems should be simple so everyone understands how, why, and when people will be rewarded. Rewards should be timely and well publicized—perhaps involving some form of ceremony. And rewards should be given with the involvement of senior management so that employees will know that their efforts are being recognized where it counts. Usually it is best to have a combination of individual and group performance measurements so that individual initiative is rewarded as well as collective results.

While every company will have its own reward and recognition system, the following are some of the basic outcomes that can be rewarded:

- perceptions of stakeholders
- bottom-line impacts of relationship building
- success of collaborative projects
- ethical behavior
- positive support for the growth and development of others

A variety of compensation systems can be put in place to motivate collaborative behavior. Profit sharing and other forms of employee ownership can foster a commitment to collaboration and relationship building. The organization must also be willing to monitor and respond to noncollaborative behavior. Such behavior needs to be confronted and dealt with promptly to minimize backsliding. Through dialogue, negotiation, and/or imposition of a new order by senior management, those values can be encouraged. A combination, carrot-and-stick approach will be likely to work best. In this approach, rewards and structures are put in place to support cooperation, and at the same time, performance evaluations are revised to increase accountability for building strong relationships with key stakeholder groups.

Risk Taking and Experimentation

Developing mutually beneficial stakeholder relationships takes time and some element of risk on the part of the organization and the individual employee. A corporate culture that encourages risk taking and experimentation will provide a nurturing environment for the growth of these relationships. To encourage risk taking, an organization should become aware of roadblocks and remove them where possible, patiently develop relationships, learn from mistakes and failures, and foster open communications.

Managers also must empower their employees to identify and build relationships with other stakeholders, help form cross-functional teams, and facilitate access to information and resources.

How Ready Is Your Organization?

Most organizations are still in the midst of a transition from the old-style hierarchical organization to a "flatter," more egalitarian, high-involvement organization. Total Quality Management (TQM), one of the most influential management theories in the past two decades, has left a legacy of teams and processes that support collaboration. Cross-functional teams were created to evaluate and improve internal business processes. Members of these teams became more adept at problem solving, brainstorming, and managing group dynamics.

Many companies have also adopted at least some of the principles contained in Peter Senge's book *The Fifth Discipline.* The essential elements of the "learning organization" provide fertile ground for collaboration. Systems thinking, personal mastery, mental models, shared vision, and team learning—the five disciplines advocated by Senge—help to generate employee commitment, an expanded capacity to learn, and the ability to communicate openly and with a spirit of enquiry rather than judgment.

Both TQM and the learning organization set the stage for collaboration beyond customers to external stakeholders. However, for many companies the internal realignment process is far from complete. Some organizational structures and systems are in place to support collaboration, while others are missing. Similarly, while some individuals working within organizations have developed the skills and motivation to participate as productive members of teams or collaborative groups, others haven't.

Aligning internal systems and structures requires an ongoing effort. No organization will ever be completely ready for collaboration because organizational readiness is multidimensional. Senior management must visibly and consistently support stakeholder collaboration, employees must understand their role in relationship building, multiway communications systems must be accessible, and rewards and recognition must be tied to the success of stakeholder relationships, not just to short-term financial indicators.

COLLABORATION READINESS ASSESSMENT GUIDE

To determine how ready your organization is to begin building collaborative relationships, consider the following questions:

1. Does senior management believe relationship building is important to bottom-line success? How is this demonstrated? *(Readiness indicators: Social concerns and responsibilities are included in the corporate mission statement; compensation of senior managers is tied to the strength of relationships with key stakeholder groups; resources are allocated to relationship-building activities.)*

2. What percentage of your CEO's time is spent communicating about building relationships with stakeholders? *(Readiness indicators: The CEO spends time in informal and formal conversations with staff, emphasizes relationship building in internal and external speeches, and participates in relationship-building processes with external stakeholders.)*

3. Do employees know who your organization's key stakeholders are and what their role is in building relationships with those groups? *(Readiness indicators: Priority stakeholders are identified by the company; relationship building is a part of job descriptions; a stakeholder feedback/audit process is in place.)*

4. Does your organization's corporate culture support collaboration through broad participation and shared decision making? *(Readiness indicators: The company uses cross-functional teams, offers profit sharing plans, and has a "flat" organizational structure.)*

5. To what extent is information shared within your organization? *(Readiness indicators: Financial information is disseminated to staff with appropriate training; information systems permit information sharing; easily accessible records of deliberations, policy, and decisions exist.)*

6. Are formal and informal communication and collaboration among staff encouraged? *(Readiness indicators: Physical space is available to hold informal conversations; e-mail and other group communication systems are accessible and used; internal newsletters are widely read and informative.)*

7. Does the corporate culture respect the needs and values of individuals, for example, through diversity, anti-discrimination, or family-friendly policies? *(Readiness indicators: A wide range of policies and*

benefits exist that are perceived by staff to be progressive and of value; staff turnover is low.)

8. Are components of the social mission reflected in the decisions made at all levels of the organization? *(Readiness indicators: The organization has measurable social goals that are reported on publicly.)*

9. Are organizational systems set up or redesigned to support the social mission? *(Readiness indicators: Managers and staff are accountable for action on the social mission either through departmental goals and results or individual performance-appraisal processes.)*

10. Are individuals recognized and rewarded for collaborative initiatives? *(Readiness indicators: Stories about collaborative initiatives are printed in corporate newsletters; individual and group pay-for-performance schemes are in place; 360-degree feedback mechanisms are available so employees can comment on the actions of superiors.)*

11. Does the organization's structure permit the right people (those affected and/or knowledgeable) to work together on tasks? *(Readiness indicators: The organization uses effective teamwork and rewards for team performance.)*

12. Do individuals have the skills they need to pursue collaborative goals? *(Readiness indicators: The staff has access to training on topics such as meeting planning, dialogue, and facilitation.)*

13. Are your company's policies geared to the long-term success of your clients or to your firm's short-term profits? *(Readiness indicators: Information is shared with key clients; scheduling is flexible to meet client needs.)*

14. Does your company know why clients are happy or unhappy with your company's services? What steps have been taken to find out? *(Readiness indicators: Regular open-ended customer surveys are taken; feedback meetings take place between senior managers and key clients at regular intervals.)*

Identifying Gaps and Inconsistencies

An employee attitude survey and a review of existing structures, systems, and policies can help to further refine the answers to the questions above and identify where changes are needed.

The information can be used to build senior management support for stakeholder collaboration, map out a process for addressing gaps and inconsistencies, and identify areas where new policies or programs are needed such as training for staff, policies governing resources for partnerships, or a review of community-relations strategies and budgets.

The results can also be used as important input into a process for developing the company's social mission. Knowing more about employee attitudes and values related to the company's social responsibilities and their role in building stakeholder relationships can help you or others in your organization plan an appropriate process for developing a corporate social mission and goals.

The following are three tasks involved in assessing and evaluating the state of collaboration within your organization:

- *Employee Attitude Survey:* An employee survey can provide useful information about employee attitudes toward collaboration and employee awareness and understanding of relationship building approaches and techniques. Various research techniques can be used, ranging from a self-completed questionnaire distributed to all employees to a series of focus groups with a sample of employees or a series of in-depth interviews with employees from all levels of the organization. The choice of which technique to use will depend on your time frame, budget, and the size of your organization.

- *Review of Corporate Systems, Policies, and Practices:* A review of corporate practices and policies related to relationships with key stakeholder groups such as employees, suppliers, and communities provides an indication of where the organization has placed the greatest effort and attention and where more effort is needed. Usually, companies have well-developed employee relations policies and a host of practices that support collaboration between employees. Policies governing relationships with external stakeholders such as suppliers and community members are often less developed.

- *Identifying Gaps and Inconsistencies:* With the results of the employee survey and the review of policies and programs, you should be able to identify any major gaps and inconsistencies in policies and practices. This information will help determine what needs to be changed to foster collaboration.

Organizational Transformation and Change Processes

Collaboration represents a new way of thinking and operating for most organizations. Slowly, internal systems and structures are changed to support this new way of being. Employees are more involved in decision-making, cross-functional teams become commonplace, corporate reward systems recognize the value of cooperation and group performance, and multiway communication occurs without being constrained by hardware, software, or hierarchies. The transition to a more collaborative organization also takes place at the individual level as managers and employees grapple with old paradigms and develop new mind-sets as well as new skill-sets.

This transformation process will require a major effort for most organizations. While the subject of organizational transformation and managing change is a field of study in itself, because of its importance to this book, I will introduce some key concepts and a few of the change methodologies that are most suited to moving organizations in the direction of collaboration.

Keep in mind that most organizational change efforts fail to produce expected results because businesses don't cope well with the emotional aspects of change. Organizations must involve their staff in creating a desirable and attainable vision and then support employees to make changes happen. Managerial tasks such as planning, budgeting, organizing, staffing, controlling, and problem solving, while important, are not the keys to successfully facilitating a strategic transformation or change process.

WHOLE SYSTEM CHANGE PROCESSES

Traditional change processes are slow and often only partially successful. Top-down decisions or those made by committees result in resistance, cynicism, and apathy on the part of employees. Whole system change methods are, on the other hand, multistakeholder approaches by definition. They are successful in bringing about organizational change because they transcend the following conventional boundaries in organizations:

- the *vertical* boundaries between management levels, positions, and rank

- the *horizontal* boundaries between departments, functions, and disciplines (often referred to as "silos")
- the *external* boundaries that separate employees from their customers, suppliers, communities, and regulators
- the *geographic/cultural* boundaries that may exist in geographically dispersed organizations relating to nations, cultures, language, and markets[16]

As Myriam Laberge, president of *Breakthroughs* UNLIMITED, a firm specializing in change processes that support collaboration, says:

> When the people on the front lines, along with middle managers and executives, hear directly from their customers, suppliers, regulators, and communities and together consider the changing external context and the need for change, a common database of information is created from which people can make wise and informed decisions. Such collaborative decisions may relate to how to redesign business processes to best serve customers, what new products and services to develop in response to new opportunities and changing market conditions, and how to re-organize work and jobs for high performance and greater job satisfaction. Involvement and participation of the "whole system" results in much greater buy-in and better overall action plans for successful and faster implementation. In today's competitive world, these pay-offs far outweigh the upfront cost of multistakeholder participation.[17]

VARIOUS TOOLS AND APPROACHES

There are various tools that can be used to help make the transition to a more collaborative organization. Many of the leading-edge approaches focus on the whole organization. Some of these "whole system technologies" include Real-Time Strategic Change, Future Search, Open Space, the Conference Model, and Dialogue. While these methods are described in detail in a number of books, they are introduced here to give you a sense of which methods are most useful for fostering collaboration.

Future Search, Real-Time Strategic Change, and Open Space bring together employees from all levels and parts of the organization to consider a common database of information. In order for the change process to be sustained through the inevitable stress and struggles, most employees must agree that change is absolutely necessary. Zeroing in on market and competitive realities, potential crises, or major opportunities helps to create a common understanding of the need for change. In some cases, external stakeholders such as suppliers, customers, or community representatives also participate so that all viewpoints and areas of expertise are present. The large group generates a "big picture" view of reality that serves as the basis for a plan for implementing change across the organization.

Out of such large group processes come action plans that are generated by the participants. They are practical and concrete. Because of the high level of participation, everyone takes responsibility for making the organization's change effort a success.

Just as all collaborative initiatives involve participants' letting go of control, these large group processes also commit an organization's leadership to following the views of the staff expressed at the sessions. The process itself demonstrates trust—that participants will put aside narrow self-interest to identify what will be the best for the organization and that the group will come up with quality decisions.

While the various whole system technologies share a basic philosophy of participation, information sharing, discovering common ground, and developing action plans, their methods are different to serve different objectives. There are three broad objectives: (1) creation of a vision of a desired future, (2) work redesign, and (3) discussion and decision making.

At the beginning of a change process, when an organization is developing a vision for a more collaborative organization, methods like Real-Time Strategic Change or Future Search are most appropriate. If one business unit is trying to redesign its work processes, the Conference Model may be best. To facilitate discussion and decision making, either about whether collaboration makes sense or about opportunities to build collaborative networks, the Open Space method may be ideal. A formal process of Dialogue may also be useful.

The following is a brief overview of each technology.

REAL-TIME STRATEGIC CHANGE

The purpose of many Real-Time Strategic Change (RTSC) events is to identify a preferred future and a path to get there with the whole organization, including customers, suppliers, and other stake-holders in the room. This method, developed by Dannemiller-Tyson & Associates, involves a three-day event with groups ranging in size from fifty to five hundred or more. Before the session, a draft or "strawman" strategy may be developed by a leadership or design team. During the session it is critically evaluated and may be refined or completely changed by participants.

The participants, through self-managed small groups, assess their organization and engage in a very powerful "Valentines" exercise, giving feedback to others in different parts of the organization about how to improve functioning. The last day is spent in system-wide action planning.

FUTURE SEARCH

Like RTSC, the purpose of Future Search is to create a future vision. This method was developed by Marvin Weisbord and Sandra Janoff based on the "Preferred Futuring" methodology of Ron Lippitt and the "Search Conference" methodology of Fred and Merrelyn Emery. Groups of thirty-five to eighty participants explore the past, present, and future and engage in a search for common ground. This methodology is particularly relevant for community building and for bringing together a multitude of stakeholder interests.

THE CONFERENCE MODEL FOR ACCELERATED WORK REDESIGN

Developed by Dick and Emily Axelrod, the Conference Model is also based on search conference principles.[18] This method consists of a series of two-day conferences, held three or more weeks apart, through which an organization can redesign a process, one unit, or the whole organization. Conferences of forty to eighty people focus on customer/vision, sector/technical analysis, design, and implementation. Special groups called Data Assist Teams work between meetings to involve everyone in the larger organization who has not been a direct participant in the process.

OPEN SPACE

Open Space is the least structured and most democratic of the large-group technologies. It was developed by Harrison Owen. In the Open Space method, participants create the agenda for the one- to three-day event in "real time" around the issues and opportunities of a focus question. This technology releases organizational energy and allows participants to take responsibility to create the results they desire. The method is unparalleled in its ability to transcend boundaries because it enables people with shared interests to come together through passionate dialogue to create new possibilities that eventually culminate in action plans. Open Space groups can range from twenty to two thousand.

DIALOGUE

Often attributed to David Bohm, dialogue has its roots in aboriginal cultures, Quaker tradition, and even gestalt therapy. Dialogue has been defined as "a sustained collective inquiry into the processes, assumptions, and certainties that compose everyday experience."[19] A formal process of dialogue can be used to facilitate change by increasing understanding and commitment to common goals among employees and other stakeholders. This method is particularly powerful in helping to transcend external and cultural or geographic boundaries.

Dialogue is aimed at developing collective intelligence by vigorously exploring individual and collective assumptions, personal predispositions, and the nature of a shared set of ideas. Its significance is highlighted when it is compared with discussion and consensus building. The purpose of discussion is to break things down into parts, to express views about what is right and wrong, and to try to influence and change the opinions of others. Consensus-building attempts to find common ground without exploring or altering underlying patterns of meaning.

Dialogue, on the other hand, asks participants to suspend attachments and particular points of view so that deeper levels of listening, synthesis, and meaning can evolve. Using dialogue, group members learn to communicate with respect, say what is on their minds, listen to and reflect on what others are saying, and decipher the deeper meaning behind opinions expressed.

According to management consultants Fred Kofman and Peter Senge, the dialogue process creates a "field of alignment" between the values and ideas of group members. With this alignment in understanding and values comes the power and the will to imagine new solutions and to bring them into being.

Why Is Dialogue Valuable in Developing Collaborative Stakeholder Relationships?

Dialogue between a multiplicity of interests and perspectives is necessary and beneficial for a number of reasons. It allows groups to

- tap the collective intelligence of all participants
- evolve a new set of values and perspectives
- understand each other's different experiences and backgrounds
- generate innovative ideas and solutions
- sort through ethical issues and areas of potential conflict
- create a common language, set of assumptions, and a collaborative process that works
- develop stronger, trusting relationships

SUSPENDING JUDGMENT—A KEY ELEMENT OF DIALOGUE

One of the great strengths of dialogue is that it allows groups of people who don't know each other well to weave a common fabric. To avoid polarizing the conversation, dialogue asks participants to suspend their reactions to what other people say, reflect on their own feelings, and wait before responding. It has been found that suspending judgment and focusing on understanding one's own response before reacting allows members of the group to build a shared sense of meaning that makes much higher levels of mutual understanding and creative thinking possible.

CLARIFYING ASSUMPTIONS CREATES A JOINT FIELD OF VISION

Dialogue is also based on the idea that behind everyone's comments and perceptions are assumptions. If those assumptions can be clarified, individuals will often reassess and modify their own beliefs and desires. Then deeper values and interests can be uncovered and a joint field of vision created. From this joint field of vision, the group is able to solve problems and generate innovative solutions.

COMMITTING TO OPEN AND CLEAR COMMUNICATION

The third basic tenet of dialogue is the commitment to open and honest communication. To develop a shared purpose and a sense of the "we," participants must be willing to

- put all their "cards on the table"
- reveal what they think, feel, and hope for
- actively listen to what others are saying
- reflect on what they have heard before speaking
- treat conflict as an opportunity for learning
- be fully present and attend to all levels of experience
- hold a deep concern for others in the group
- be willing to experiment with and test new ideas in the face of uncertainty

Designing a Dialogue Session

To realize the most profound benefits of dialogue, there must be enough energy and commitment to sustain the dialogue process for at least several months. Usually there is no set agenda, but perhaps a theme or focus like "working together." During a dialogue session, space should be arranged to promote a feeling of equality with chairs set in a circle.

Someone trained in the dialogue method should take on the role of facilitator. After the facilitator describes the concept of dialogue and the ground rules for communication, each person has an opportunity, but is not required, to say what is on his or her mind. In this way, people have an opportunity to see how others are thinking and feeling about critical matters and about each other.

As Peter Senge and others at the MIT Center for Organizational Learning have observed, "We are finding that the more we organize around dialogue, and the less we plan out elaborate agendas, the more we accomplish."

Case Study: Maintaining Collective Vision Using Dialogue[20]
Odwalla, Inc. is a California-based manufacturer of natural fruit juices with more than six hundred employees working at twenty-three offices in seven states. Thirty to forty Odwalla staff

meet every two months for eight-hour dialogue sessions. The broad goals of the sessions are

- to listen and learn—to tap into and benefit from the collective wisdom, unique perspectives, and insights of people from every area of the company
- to see the big picture—to get a clearer picture of the interests, values, and experiences of Odwalla staff and in so doing gain a better understanding of the Odwalla corporate culture and the relationship between the company and the society as a whole
- to practice communication—to learn to communicate better with each other by listening attentively and thinking before responding

The company has found that the process of dialogue helped it maintain its mission and vision during a period of dramatic growth. Dialogue has also provided other unexpected benefits. For example, it was instrumental in helping staff cope with the crisis stemming from the apparent contamination of Odwalla apple juice with a strain of *E. coli* bacteria in October 1996.

Although the dialogue sessions were halted during the crisis, participants reported that their previous experience with dialogue helped them remain connected to each other and to their common goals. The strategic marketing communications group, which is responsible for communicating with the public, met on its own for two dialogue sessions. The group found that it provided a forum for building and expressing mutual support and for working through some of the issues members faced during the crisis.

Participants report that the benefits of the dialogue sessions include

- a bridging of the power and authority gaps between staff from different levels of the organization
- feeling connected to employees from other offices
- integrating personal and corporate vision into their work

Developing a
Stakeholder Strategy

Strategy is the way a company defines its business and links together the only two resources that really matter in today's economy: knowledge and relationships.

—R. Normann and R. Ramirez, 1993

Building stakeholder relationships is becoming more challenging. As the boundaries around and within corporations become more diffuse, the number and complexity of relationships increases. In addition, the potential for inconsistencies and errors of judgment grows as more employees are empowered to take on responsibilities for initiating and managing relationships with external stakeholders. These factors increase the need for a consistent and effective stakeholder strategy.

This chapter outlines a process for developing such a strategy. By following the steps outlined in this chapter, you will be able to answer the following important questions:

- What are the strengths, weaknesses, and gaps in our existing network of stakeholder relationships?

- Who are our priority stakeholders?

- What do we expect to receive from each priority stakeholder group? What are we prepared to give?

- What do our stakeholders expect from our organization? What are they prepare to give?

- Are they interested in establishing closer ties? Do we have common concerns and interests?

- What are the limiting conditions and requirements for successful relationship building, including resources and time?

- Who will champion relationship building within our organization? Who else needs to be involved? What actions need to be taken?

Stakeholder-Focused Corporate Strategy

You will recall that one of the key features of the model of corporate-stakeholder relations described in chapter 3 was the notion that corporate strategy, among other things, defines how a company manages its explicit and implicit contracts with stakeholders. It defines what the company expects to receive from its stakeholder relationships and what it is prepared to give. This stakeholder-oriented view of strategy differs sharply from the traditional view that strategic plans should focus mostly on financial goals and initiatives designed to improve financial performance.

A stakeholder-oriented approach to corporate strategy makes more sense today than in the past because companies depend more on their stakeholder relationships to ensure financial success. To ensure long-term success, a company must manage the increasingly important intangibles that drive financial performance, like employee know-how, the quality of relationships with suppliers, customer satisfaction, and corporate reputation. Today more than 60 percent of a company's value is tied up with intangibles rather than hard assets like machinery or land.[1] This figure rises even higher in knowledge-based industries.

A recent study involving five of Canada's largest and most progressive companies indicates that a stakeholder-oriented approach to corporate strategy-making is becoming more common. All five companies included a broad array of stakeholders in their strategic plans. For instance, at Nova Corporation, an integrated natural gas services and petrochemicals company headquartered in Calgary, Alberta, strategy focuses on four key stakeholder groups: shareholders, customers, employees, and communities. Senior management and members of the board of directors believe that to fulfill the company's vision and achieve long-term profitability, employees and management must excel at meeting the needs of these groups. Over the long term, they believe that financial results are driven by superior performance for customers, employees, and the community. Accordingly, the company's strategy includes specific goals for each stakeholder group including the following:

- *shareholders*—provide above-average returns compared with the Toronto Stock Exchange 100 Index over a five-year period
- *customers*—demonstrate continuous improvement in overall satisfaction based on items such as reliable service, low cost, and flexibility of service
- *employees*—achieve a high level of performance on twelve factors including satisfaction, employee wellness, and safety
- *community*—be a leader in developing mutually supportive relationships in the communities where the company operates[2]

The goals are based on Nova's understanding of various economic and social forces operating in its environment, including the priorities and interests of its stakeholders plus, of course, the company's core values and overall mission.

What Is a Stakeholder Strategy?

A stakeholder strategy provides a road map for an organization to forge new relationships with strategically important stakeholders and also to reorient or extend existing relationships. It is a major component of an overall corporate strategic plan. The stakeholder strategy should identify key stakeholders, strategic priorities, and goals for each stakeholder group and outline an action plan for each. The strategy is a work in progress that needs to be extended and updated as relationships develop. Ideally, its focus should be on a medium-term period of two to five years.

The following are the major steps involved in developing a stakeholder strategy. Each step will be discussed in depth in the rest of this chapter.

Assessing Stakeholder Relationships

EXISTING RELATIONSHIP NETWORKS

Companies often have an entrenched network of stakeholder relationships. Some relationships may be mutually beneficial and strong.

Table 7
Strategy Development

Tasks	Tools/Method	Results
• inventory and assess existing relationships	• inventory questionnaire	• status report on current relationships completed
• benchmark best practices	• RB Strategy Group workshop	• "best practices" established
• meet with stakeholders	• environmental scan	• priorities identified
• refine goals and prepare strategy	• informal dialogue with stakeholders	• views and needs of potential partners understood
• set up internal structures	• stakeholder team meetings	• goals clarified
• begin action planning		• stakeholder teams formed
		• strategy and action plans put in place

Others will likely be weak or nonexistent. How can this existing network of relationships be used to build more strategic collaborative alliances? How can these relationships be strengthened and, if necessary, reoriented toward collaboration rather than defensiveness, opportunity seeking rather than buffering? How can larger companies ensure that relationship building is consistent from one department to the next and that staff members aren't separately trying to build relationships with the same partner organizations?

To answer these questions, a company first needs to identify its existing network by drawing up a list of stakeholder relationships and then conducting an inventory and assessment of those relationships. Often the network is more extensive than it appears at first glance. This may be because these relationships, often existing at the middle management level, are not valued or officially sanctioned. In fact, they may even be perceived as antithetical to competitive business operations in that the relationships depend on sharing information or resources.

However, to get the job done, most effective managers have informal relationships with their company's stakeholders. Community relations managers consult informally with leaders of prominent citizens groups to keep abreast of emerging issues and concerns. Government relations staff keep in touch with policymakers to ensure corporate interests are understood and taken account of. Production managers liaise regularly with their suppliers to ensure that component parts can be delivered on time. Often the effectiveness of a middle manager is directly proportional to the quality of his or her stakeholder relationships.

DEVELOPING A LONG LIST OF STAKEHOLDERS

Before the inventory is conducted, a list of company stakeholders should be compiled that is as specific as possible. (See table 8 for a sample list of stakeholders.) For example, community stakeholders might include a citizen's group representing neighbors of a company facility or executive members of the sports organizations that depend on the company for donations. Industry stakeholders can include major suppliers and business partners. Employee stakeholders can include new employees as well as still-active retirees.

Table 8
Sample List of Primary (p) and Secondary (s) Stakeholders

Owners
- shareholders/investors (p)
- employee pension fund holders (p)
- mutual fund managers (s)

Customers
- individual buyers (p)
- ethnic niche markets (p)
- consumer media spokespersons (s)
- consumer associations (s)

Employees
- new employees (p)
- older, long-term employees (p)
- minority groups (p)
- retirees (p)
- employees with families (p)
- unions (s)

Industry
- suppliers (p)
- competitors (s)
- industry associations (s)
- industry opinion leaders (s)

Community
- residents living near company sites (p)
- residents' associations (s)
- chambers of commerce (s)
- charity organizations (s)
- schools and universities (s)
- special interest groups (s)

Environment/Nonhuman Species/Future Generations
- the natural environment (p)
- nonhuman species (p)
- future generations (p)
- scientists (s)
- environmental activist groups (s)

Media
- media spokespersons (s)
- columnists (s)

Government Regulators
- federal policymakers (s)
- state/provincial officials (s)
- local officials (s)

Defining customer stakeholder groups can be relatively straightforward. Often the company's business plan and annual report are the best places to start searching. Look at where the company spends the bulk of its resources. Review its major initiatives to see which groups were affected. For example, the 1996 business plan of a large bank in Seattle indicated that the company was attempting to woo new immigrants as customers. The plan indicated that the bank devoted 40 percent of its marketing budget to sponsorship and advertising directed at the Taiwan-American community. Lesser amounts were spent attracting immigrants from other, smaller ethnic communities.

This tells us that ethnic communities are an important customer stakeholder group for the bank, with greatest priority given to Taiwanese-American immigrants. It is possible to develop even more specific definitions, for example, by considering the length of time the Taiwanese customers have lived in the United States. Those that have lived in North America longer will have different financial interests and needs than those who have just arrived. One group may be of greater priority to the bank than the other and should be identified as such to maximize the effectiveness of relationship-building initiatives later on.

CONDUCTING A STAKEHOLDER INVENTORY

A questionnaire can be used to collect information on existing relationships from a broad cross section of staff members who deal with the company's major stakeholders. The questionnaire should include the following types of questions:

- Which of these stakeholder groups do you believe has the greatest impact on our company?
- Which ones does our company affect the most?
- How would you rate the state of our relationship with these groups (nonexistent, weak, moderate, strong, very strong)?
- What are the benefits of these relationship for our company and for you personally?
- What are the benefits for the partner organizations and for partners as individuals?
- What are the relationship's strengths and weaknesses?
- Are there any threats to the continuation of the relationship or any unresolved problems or barriers?
- Does the relationship offer large, moderate, or limited opportunities? Describe the possible opportunities.

- What would be needed to build a stronger, more collaborative relationship?

- Are there any other important stakeholder groups that we need to build relationships with? Why are these groups important? List contact names for these organizations.

- What future role would you like to play in building or strengthening relationships with stakeholders?

Based on the survey results, strengths and weaknesses and gaps in existing relationships should be identified. In addition to helping to identify areas where relationships are lacking, this data can help to sort out which relationships are fine as they are and which ones need to be strengthened. Barriers and opportunities should also be highlighted.

IDENTIFY NEW AND STRATEGICALLY IMPORTANT STAKEHOLDER RELATIONSHIPS

To identify new and strategically important stakeholder relationships, think of your business environment as an ecosystem. To do this, put yourself in the shoes of a competitor and think about who its important stakeholders are. Talk to your suppliers and ask them where they think new opportunities for alliances might lie.

By identifying and forming cooperative partnerships with others in their ecosystem, companies can, for example, meet emerging customer needs using new technologies or open up new markets using innovative distribution channels. As Richard Normann and Rafael Ramirez suggest in their seminal article on value constellations, published in the *Harvard Business Review*, "the reinvention of any business constellation is at least partly a matter of thinking through the social implications of change."[3]

In their book *Co-Opetition*, authors Adam Brandenburger and Barry Nalebuff also offer some interesting ideas about how companies can identify new stakeholders and sources of opportunity.[4] They suggest that companies can open up new opportunities by cooperating with complementary businesses. They use term "complementor" to describe other businesses whose products or services makes a company's own products more attractive. Think about mustard as being a complementor to hot dogs or auto insurance to new cars. Based on game theory, the authors suggest that while competition may be the best strategy when it comes to dividing up the pie, cooperation works better when there is potential for making the pie bigger.

By collecting and reviewing additional background information, a company can identify emerging opportunities in its "business ecosystem" that could be tapped through new alliances and partnerships. Information on the following can be useful:

- customer characteristics
- competitor practices and networks
- new technology
- demographic patterns
- social trends
- new government policies

At the end of this process you should have narrowed down your list to about six to ten priority stakeholders, taking into account corporate strategies, emerging markets or opportunities, and areas of potential weakness or liability.

Benchmarking Best Practices

Organizations can learn a great deal by studying "best practices" with respect to collaboration both within and outside their companies. Begin the benchmarking process by identifying where collaboration is most important for your organization and where you have the greatest scope for improvement. Within most companies, there are groups of employees who collaborate successfully on projects, in some cases in conjunction with external organizations. With some informal exploration, you will be able to find these "pockets" of high-intensity collaboration and discover what makes them work.

Consider other companies in your industry. Some profitable, well-managed companies will also be known to have created long-term, mutually beneficial relationships with their stakeholders. Finally, there may be other companies outside the industry that have developed innovative, collaborative practices that could be relevant to your company.

A benchmarking program typically involves determining what to benchmark and who to benchmark against and collecting all the information that will help to do this. The purpose of the benchmarking process is to assess the gap between what you actually do and what a study of best practices says you should do.

Case Study: Identifying Potential Partners in the Music Business

The following vignette describes how a small fictitious record company develops collaborative relationships with other industry partners and customers to meet mutual goals.

Circle Records is a mail-order music distribution company. At its latest strategic planning session, world beat music was identified as an increasingly popular genre with a large number of potential customers. The company has a small roster of world beat music titles that it would like to expand. A series of focus groups with existing and potential customers showed that those customers would purchase music through the mail-order channel.

Circle Records decided that as part of its marketing strategy, it needed to develop closer ties with customers who like world beat music and that to be effective without a large advertising budget, it needed to work closely with other organizations that also were linked to this customer group.

A team was formed to spearhead this relationship-building effort. The director of human resources was selected as one key member of the team, at least partly because she regularly attends world beat concerts and is an avid fan. Another member of the team from the sales department was selected because he was familiar with the language and culture of world beat music, given that he worked as a volunteer for many summers at folk festivals across the United States.

The team reviewed market information on the world beat buyer group and identified several organizations that were well connected with that group including the Folk Festival Society, the World Beat Music Performers Association, and numerous Celtic music appreciation clubs located in and around major North American cities.

By identifying and contacting leaders of these organizations, team members discovered more about their links with world beat music buyers and their immediate and long-term needs and goals. They discovered that the Folk Festival Society was interested in identifying the most popular world beat performers as part of its strategy to attract more customers to festivals. The performers association wanted to set up a hotline to publicize concerts and to provide members with feedback on popular songs, styles, and concert formats. All three organizations were interested in establishing ongoing communication with world beat music fans.

They also discovered that individual members of the Celtic Music Appreciation Club and other similar organizations across the country were interested in attending performances of Celtic music, one category of world beat music. Many also wanted to find out where they could buy their favorite CDs (compact disks) soon after release.

Circle Records recognized common interests among all of these organizations. The company decided that it would become the leader in that "business ecosystem" and create a collaborative focus between the organizations and ultimately the world beat customers. After meeting with representatives from the two partner organizations, the company decided to establish a joint web site and discussion group to provide information about upcoming concerts and CDs and tapes available from the record company and to solicit feedback from concert goers and music buyers about their preferred performers and their reaction to local concerts. As the project was planned and implemented and the relationships between the three organizations strengthened, more opportunities arose.

Informal Dialogue with Stakeholders

The next stage of relationship building involves informal dialogue with potential partners to clarify their interests and expectations and to share information about the company's goals and expectations. A further purpose is to determine their level of interest in developing a closer collaborative relationship and to identify common goals and possible areas for collaboration.

During this phase, the following types of information about potential partner organizations should be gathered if possible:

- organizational structure and history
- corporate values and management style
- strengths and weaknesses
- recent collaborative initiatives and outcomes
- similar relationships with other companies

- interest in forming closer relationships
- possible areas of collaboration

This informal consultation can take place over coffee, by phone or e-mail, or at trade shows or industry meetings. Ideally, the person initiating the contact with the partner organization should have a relationship with him or her already and be familiar with the culture of the stakeholder organization(s). This background, along with the ability to listen carefully, can help move the relationship-building initiative along.

Organizations that display similar values and culture, including human resource policies, administrative systems, and approaches to decision making, will form more effective and efficient collaborative partners.[5] A good organizational fit, in addition to a strategic fit, enhances the extent to which organizations can get along and capitalize on the synergies that are critical to building a dynamic long-term relationship.

An organization's reputation also affects its capacity to form collaborative relationships. Each partner's perceptions of the other's management ability, product or service quality, and financial situation will affect the partner's willingness to form collaborative relationships and the speed with which a cohesive partnership can be established. The initiator of the collaborative venture will have already assessed the reputation of partner organizations in the narrowing-down process. Those that are approached will also likely consider the reputation of the initiating organization in their decision about whether to begin the dialogue.

EXTENDING RELATIONSHIPS WITH EXISTING PARTNERS

Collaborative partnerships are easier to establish if the organizations and/or the individual members have worked together before. This experience helps build an understanding of each other's capabilities and resources. It also increases trust, one of the key ingredients in successful collaborative relationships. Existing or previous economic and social ties help the relationship develop more quickly and efficiently than when the parties are strangers.

When exploring the potential to collaborate with an existing partner, take the time to review past projects and clear up any misunderstandings. Also, learn from past experiences with the partner, and clarify how interests, needs, and capabilities may have changed.

> **Exhibit 1: Clarifying Expectations with Known Partners**
> - take time to review the past relationship
> - identify what made it work well
> - identify what could have been improved
> - learn from the experience
> - let go of negative feelings
> - share current information about personal goals and capabilities
> - clarify the level of commitment both parties want

INITIATING A NEW COLLABORATIVE RELATIONSHIP

A relationship with a new partner organization will develop more slowly and will most often begin with a small informal project that requires little reliance on trust because it involves little risk. As these experiences evolve and more complex projects are undertaken, trust develops, the relationship deepens, and commitment to the partnership increases.

In situations where a relationship does not already exist, information about potential partner organizations can be gathered initially through discussions with others who know the organizations and by reviewing secondary sources such as annual reports, industry publications, and media clipping files. With smaller organizations, direct contact should be made with the CEO or executive director. In larger companies, contact should be initiated with a vice president or person in charge of alliances.

The purpose of the first few meetings is to enable participants to share and receive information about each other's organizations and to get to know each other as individuals and as potential partners. Senior managers from both organizations should attend, along with the "champion" of the relationship and one or two others from each organization who are knowledgeable about the problem or opportunity area.

Usually, at the first one or two meetings, when people don't know one another, they will operate "in role." That is, they will focus on conveying a positive impression of themselves and their organization. The attribution of motives by participants at this stage depends on the history of the dealings between the organizations and the reputation of individuals. Unspoken questions will arise, such as

- What are the motives of the other individuals?
- What are the interests of the organizations they represent?
- What do they have that would be useful to me personally and to our organization?
- Do I like and respect these people?
- Are they competent?
- Have we established enough trust to proceed?
- Are they committed?
- Is our organization committed to proceeding?
- Are our corporate cultures compatible?
- Do I trust them enough to invest the time in building a relationship?

Until a sufficient level of trust develops, it may be necessary to formalize agreements between the parties with a binding contract. While it is recognized that "contracts don't make relationships, people do," in some cases a more formalized agreement can help pave the way toward more open communication.

Exhibit 2: Do's and Don'ts for First Meetings

- Do be honest about your capabilities.
- Do plan ahead to ensure the appropriate people are at the table.
- Do allow time to share information about each organization's strategic directions, culture, and needs.
- Do allow informal social time for participants to learn about each other's backgrounds and personalities.
- Do stress the importance of everyone's contribution.
- Do ensure that one person with the necessary process skills takes on the role of facilitator.
- Don't set up unrealistic expectations by promising more than you or your organization can deliver.
- Don't identify one or more of the participants as the "expert."

Establishing Stakeholder Goals

Once an organization has some understanding of the strengths and weaknesses of its existing relationships, has identified its priority stakeholders, and has initiated a dialogue with those groups, it can begin to develop more specific stakeholder goals.

Ben and Jerry's, one of North America's best known values-driven companies, has developed goals for each of its major stakeholder groups based on the company's mission and business strategy. The mission and business strategy are the reference point for these stakeholder-specific goals in that they define what the company expects to receive and what it is prepared to give. These goals are also used in the "audit" of the company's social performance.

Case Study: Developing Stakeholder Goals

Vermont-based Ben and Jerry's Homemade, Inc., has an overall corporate mission to "make, distribute, and sell the finest quality all-natural ice cream and related products in a wide variety of innovative flavors made from Vermont dairy products." This statement is supported by stakeholder-specific social goals, such as the following goals for relationships with customers and franchisees. Ben and Jerry's also has social goals for staff, stockholders, and recipients of philanthropy.

Customers

To price our products fairly; to cover reasonable costs and earn a fair profit.

To respond to comments, complaints and concerns of customers quickly and respectfully.

To describe and promote our products truthfully.

To engage customers in conversation about our products and our social goals.

Franchisees

To maintain franchise relationships within which capable independent business owners can run profitable, sustainable enterprises.

To be clear with franchisees about their role in the Ben and Jerry's mission and to provide to them consistent, useful technical and logistical support.

To make franchise shops expressions of Ben and Jerry's commitment to quality, customer satisfaction, fun and social purpose.[6]

Setting Up Internal Structures

RELATIONSHIP-BUILDING STRATEGY GROUP

New internal systems and structures may be required to spearhead the relationship-building initiative. Senior level managers and ideally the CEO will be involved in assessing collaboration as a strategic direction and then, if a decision is made to proceed, in setting major corporate goals for the collaboration initiative. A relationship-building strategy group should be formed to oversee the development of the relationship-building strategy. The group should include senior managers from the departments that deal with the major stakeholder groups, including human resources, community relations, product development, operations, marketing, and finance.

An important task for the relationship-building strategy group is to facilitate cross-departmental information sharing and feedback so that people who are actively involved in relationship building with specific stakeholder organizations have input into the strategy from the beginning. This group should also coordinate the review of the corporate social mission, values, and ethics, ideally with a cross section of employees.

The relationship-building strategy group should develop the priority stakeholder list based on the results of the inventory and assessment and on the consideration of strategically important new relationships.

STAKEHOLDER TEAMS

Cross-functional teams should be created to implement relationship building with each priority stakeholder group. There should be some crossover between the members of the strategy group and the stakeholder teams. These cross-functional teams should ideally include individuals who already have relationships with the stakeholder groups and are committed to moving toward closer, more collaborative alliances.

These teams will be responsible for developing and implementing the relationship-building action plans, including meeting informally with stakeholder representatives. The teams will coordinate the on-the-ground relationship-building initiatives and will be accountable for the relationships with their stakeholder groups.

In the following case study, you will see how a cross-functional task force at Levi Strauss led a two-year international communication and consultation process with key stakeholders.

Case Study: Stakeholder Consultation on Sourcing Guidelines

Foreign production practices by North American–based companies have been scrutinized by national media, unions, public interest groups, and elected officials. The American public is concerned about exploitation of workers and about the movement of jobs to Third World countries. Public criticism has focused on companies such as Nike, Wal-Mart and Levi Strauss. While some of the other companies have been more defensive, Levi Strauss developed guidelines for sourcing materials from developing countries several years ago in consultation with its staff, suppliers, and other stakeholders.

In 1991, a cross-functional task force began a two-year international communication and consultation process to identify issues related to sources, standards, and the company's existing practices.

The task force obtained regular feedback from twenty-five internal and external stakeholder groups. It also conducted research on the wages, working conditions, and benefits available to the seven hundred sewing and finishing contractors who work for Levi Strauss in more than fifty countries. The task force members considered merchandising and production needs, Levi Strauss' social responsibilities, and differing cultural values.

The guidelines, the first of their kind, were adopted in 1992. In-country managers were selected to enforce terms of engagement. Levi Strauss also provided auditor training sessions for one hundred managers, performed ongoing monitoring of contractor practices, distributed guidelines to members of the American Apparel Manufacturers Association, and shared its research with other companies.

The guidelines helped Levi Strauss ensure that its products were being made under conditions consistent with the company's commitment to corporate social responsibility and helped protect the company's reputation.

Action Planning

The information collected by the stakeholder teams can be used to develop stakeholder-specific action plans. The plans should include more specific objectives that have been revised based on discussions with potential partners, as well as roles and responsibilities, and timelines.

Once the stakeholder teams have developed their action plans, the relationship-building strategy group should review them to identify synergies and conflicts as well as the organizational systems and structures that are needed to support the collaborative efforts. Communication and coordination systems as well as mechanisms for evaluating progress and resolving conflicts should be put in place. The legal department may also be asked to look at the legal ramifications of particular alliances.

Harnessing the Power of Long-Term Relationships

There is no such thing as a long-term, no-strings, convenient, one-sided relationship. All require planning, negotiation of differences, establishment of trust and respect, and commitment to mutual benefit.

—K. Reardon and R. Spekman, 1994

There are many reasons why collaborative relationships are established and then dissolve after one or two projects or thrive in the short term but fizzle out after the first year or two. Relationships may be terminated for reasons beyond the group's control, such as a shift in organizational priorities or a change in the economy. Or the reasons may lie within the group itself. Members may not get along, people may expect too much too soon, a short-term project may be completed without deepening commitment, or excessive legal conditions may be set by parent organizations.

Like marriage, collaborative partnerships don't work for everyone. In some cases, a prospective partner may enter the alliance for self-interested reasons—for example, to obtain a better price for a product, to sell more goods or services, or to gain information and competitive advantage in the process. Others want to be the "senior" partner in the relationship and find it difficult to relinquish control over the partnership's course.

In the last chapter, we discussed how to identify your company's stakeholders, decide which ones are most important, establish a dialogue with potential partners, and develop a relationship-building strategy. The next phase involves implementing that strategy—forging new stakeholder relationships while strengthening existing ones. Keep in mind that while the focus here is on organization-to-organization collaboration, the same principles and approaches apply to collaboration initiatives within organizations.

In this chapter, we will look at what it takes to create and sustain powerful, innovative collaborative relationships. We will review the major types of collaborative relationships and the conditions that lead to collaborative action. Next, we will focus on the challenges involved in collaborative ventures and then on strategies for designing an effective collaborative process. We will address issues such as organization-to-organization compatibility, tension between autonomy and accountability, communication, trust, and conflict.

Table 9
Trust Building

Tasks	Tools/Method	Results
• exchange information • clarify expectations and perspectives • identify common goals • develop organizational structures • clarify roles and responsibilities, short-term objectives, and timelines • develop and implement "first projects" • identify and resolve areas of conflict • ensure availability of resources	• face-to-face meetings • on-line information system, e-mail • facilitated workshops • experiential events • dialogue • conflict resolution	• access to larger pool of information • increased trust • shared language and vision • more integrated relationships between organizations • innovative solutions • enhanced reputation for both organizations with successful projects

Types of Collaborative Relationships

Stakeholder collaboration can take many forms and produce a variety of results. The following chart describes the most common types of collaborative ventures involving corporations and their stakeholders.

Table 10
Types of Collaborative Relationships
Source: Adapted from B. Gray, *Collaborating: Finding Common Ground for Multiparty Problems.* (San Francisco: Jossey-Bass, 1989).

Type of Stakeholder Collaboration	Intended Result
Interfirm joint ventures	stimulate innovation, minimize risk
Supplier-customer collaboration (joint information systems, involvement of suppliers on design teams, joint product development)	improve efficiency, enhance communication, reduce costs
Corporate-community economic development	cope with economic decline, revitalize communities
Corporate-nongovernmental organization (NGO) social marketing campaigns	change social behavior and enhance corporate and NGO reputations
Corporate-special interest group action on social or environmental issue	strengthen community, solve problems, foster employee satisfaction, enhance corporate reputation
Multilateral collaboration (nations, NGOs, multinationals)	foster sustainability, achieve global management of resources, deal with trade issues
Corporate-government public policy task forces	resolve policy disputes, develop consensus on new policy directions, solve skilled labor shortages
Business-university research consortia	exchange expertise, save money on R&D
Customer representatives on design teams, in joint planning sessions	improve products, planning, and communications
Stakeholder representatives on corporate boards of directors	ensure stakeholder values and perspectives are reflected in corporate policies and plans
Nonprofit group representatives in training programs	provide a social benefit, bring new ideas into the organization
Internal collaboration across business units	reduce costs, increase innovation, improve relationships
Union-management joint committees	improve corporate performance, health and safety, working relationships

The Context for Collaborative Action

Collaboration does not occur without a great deal of effort on the part of a number of individuals and their respective organizations. Under what conditions do people who are busy meeting the demands of their own business units or organizations explore partnership opportunities? Knowing more about the conditions that foster collaborative action can help you decide how to proceed with your relationship-building initiatives.

A LAST RESORT

People often move into collaboration when all else fails or when there is no possibility to solve a problem or take advantage of an opportunity unilaterally. Collaboration is often seen as a last resort. As one collaboration expert said, "People back into the collaborative moment."

Today more business leaders recognize that singular action is no longer an option. As the boundaries between and within organizations become more diffuse and permeable, organizations must collaborate to take advantage of centralized resources through decentralized decision making. Collaborative relationships provide companies with access to new technologies, ideas, and markets—essential assets in a highly competitive, globalized economy.

CLEAR NEED AND HIGH STAKES

When a problem or opportunity is clear cut and the consequences of not taking action are severe, people are most likely to collaborate. This situation can be understood in light of the social-psychological theory of the "commons." People will work together to solve problems when conditions get bad enough to threaten continued use of a common resource but not so bad that the likelihood of resolving the problem is limited.

For instance, in the past few years people from all types of organizations across the United States have joined forces to address social problems associated with the growing tide of poverty and violence in American cities. Widespread support for collaborative processes exists now because people believe that continued inaction will lead to much more profound levels of social disintegration and that while conditions are bad, there is hope that problems can be resolved if people work together.

Collaboration between business, community, and government to resolve environmental problems is also becoming more common. For example, General Motors Corp. and British Petroleum have announced a collaborative relationship with the Washington, D.C.–based World Resources Institute to develop measures to avert global climate change.

The aim of the collaboration, called "Safe Climate, Sound Business," is to develop a long-term vision for protecting the earth's climate and producing the technologies and policies for getting there.

SELF-INTEREST

People and organizations are willing to collaborate with others if by doing so they can serve their own interests. Companies may want to establish collaborative relationships with organizations to build trust and reduce costs associated with carrying out their actions, to improve their reputation by acting in concert with stakeholder expectations, or to reduce long-term uncertainty by establishing interdependencies.

However, companies also decide to participate in collaborative processes solely to protect their own interests. For example, companies may participate in policy-development exercises with government, business, and nonprofit organizations, not so much for altruistic reasons but to ensure their point of view is heard and the interests of other stakeholders don't take precedence.

HIGH INTERDEPENDENCE

When firms recognize that their interests can be achieved best through coordination and cooperation with others and when self-interest is linked to broader community interests, willingness to collaborate increases significantly. Research shows that a high level of perceived interdependence is a prerequisite for successful collaboration.[1]

Case Study: Collaboration between First Nations and MacMillan Bloedel Limited

Since the late 1970s, First Nations in British Columbia's Nuuchah-nulth area have been concerned about forest practices, both in terms of declining employment of First Nations people in the forest industry and the damage that logging practices were causing to salmon rivers and streams. In 1993, First Nations people led an effective protest against over-harvesting in the Clayquot Sound area of coastal British Columbia. This "war in the woods," which brought international attention to British Columbia, has had a significant effect on the operations of many forest companies, including MacMillan Bloedel.

In the five years since the original protest, negotiations have been taking place between the government, forest companies, and First Nations leaders. In April 1996, after three years of negotiations, a joint-venture agreement was put in place between MacMillan Bloedel and Ma-Mook Development Corporation, a First Nations–owned development corporation. Ma-Mook and MacMillan Bloedel will jointly own and operate a logging company on provincially owned crown lands within the Clayquot Sound area of British Columbia.

As Howard Tom, chair of Ma-Mook said, "We have a vision of being organized to advance our values and interests while at the same time creating and nourishing broader relationships with the human family. Our neighbors are valued and our partnerships with a wide range of aboriginal and nonaboriginal organizations and institutions are means through which we both gain and contribute a web of mutual benefit."[2]

STRONG STAKEHOLDER GROUPS

The process of planning and implementing interorganizational projects is much more efficient when the stakeholder organizations have clearly articulated goals and values, recognized leaders, and a structure for communicating with constituents. For example, in order for MacMillan Bloedel and First Nations people to develop a collaborative agreement, the five First Nations of the Nuu-chah-nulth region needed to create a strong organizational structure to represent the economic interests of all of their people through the Ma-Mook Development Corporation.

Challenges Involved in Collaboration

Many challenges arise during the process of building effective collaborative relationships. The following are some of the most significant.

DIVERGING AIMS, INTERESTS, AND CULTURES

Individuals who come together to undertake a collaborative venture will undoubtedly come from varied backgrounds and will have different aims, language, and cultural values. In some cases, the aims of individuals will be in conflict with one another. In others, individuals may be operating from widely divergent assumptions. Without an effective process to identify and explore differences in assumptions and language and to develop mutual understanding and agreement on project objectives, the likelihood of success is limited.

This is especially true when individuals come from different sectors—corporate, government, or nonprofit organizations. Developing mutual understanding is perhaps the most important and difficult task in forging successful collaborative relationships.

SIGNIFICANT TIME COMMITMENT

One of the drawbacks of collaboration is the amount of time required to develop successful relationships with others. Time is needed for people to get to know each other, to build trust, to deal with organizational issues, to negotiate agreements, and to manage the logistics of working together.

In many cases, collaborative ventures require several attempts before they finally succeed.[3] Often when a collaborative project fails the first time, it is reborn later in a slightly different guise with a different mix of players. Ultimately, the survival of collaborative relationships depends on the ability of the collaboration to create real value for the organizations involved. With value comes commitment, and with commitment comes renewed energy and resources.

POWER AND STATUS DIFFERENCES

Collaborative ventures involving corporations and their stakeholders are plagued by problems caused by perceived and actual power and status differences between participants. As most partnerships lack preexisting decision-making structures, these arrangements, both formal and informal, must be worked out by the group.

In some corporate-nonprofit sector partnering, companies come to the table convinced that they know best how to design and manage projects. They fail to appreciate the strengths of their stakeholder partners and hence are unable to open their minds and hearts to develop creative, mutually beneficial solutions.

"It is important that both parties are equal at the table, that the corporation is not seen as the savior, but listens and helps to identify common goals," says Mary Mathieu, formerly in charge of training for the Points of Light Foundation. Mathieu notes that, in the past ten years of corporate-nonprofit sector partnering, U.S. companies have often come to the table convinced that only they knew how to design and manage social projects. "Companies have to learn how to collaborate," she stresses.

Before jumping into a partnership, Mathieu and others in her field caution that companies need to ask themselves some hard questions: "Is the issue tied closely enough to our core business strategy?" "How deep is our interest in this issue?" "Will we be able to sustain our interest and commitment in the longer term?" After carefully considering whether a firm can help a particular nonprofit accomplish its mission, it is time to talk about who is bringing what expertise to the table.

DIFFERENCES IN RESOURCES AND CAPABILITIES

Corporations often bring financial resources to the table along with expectations about how projects should be managed. The nonprofit organization may not have the financial and human resources to respond. By law, nonprofit organizations must spend virtually all their funds on program and service delivery. This leaves precious little for administration and strategic planning, professional development, or business and organizational training. Individuals in this sector are often overwhelmed by the sophisticated strategies proposed by their corporate partners.

Secondly, corporate-nonprofit sector partners may find it difficult to adapt to each other's culture and values. The competitive, "time is money" culture of the corporate world is often at odds with the more cooperative, process-oriented style of nonprofit sector organizations.

GENDER DIFFERENCES

Differences between men and women in the way they approach collaboration can both contribute to and hinder the success of a collaborative venture.[4] Researchers have found, for example, that collaborative processes led by women are characterized by higher levels of creative problem solving and a greater value placed on people rather than financial resources. Women-led processes also tend to move more quickly to shared power.[5]

Collaborative projects led by men are more likely to be influenced by the positions of power and authority held by the participants. Men also

Table 11
Issues and Solutions to Collaboration Challenges

Issues	Solutions
Different aims, interests, and cultures	• allow time for participants to get to know each other • build in a cycle of relationship-building activities followed by action • include site visits to share experiences • use an independent facilitator • clarify objectives • use dialogue to increase understanding
Power and status differences	• agree on ground rules • be aware of gender differences in collaborative style • establish fair decision-making processes • address issues of legitimacy
Tension between autonomy and accountability	• encourage ongoing communication with constituent organizations • clarify and manage host organization's expectations
Different resources and capabilities	• share resources • acknowledge contributions
Time commitment required	• discuss and agree on time commitments at the beginning • assume that the time required will be double what is anticipated
Communication challenges	• involve people with good communication/conflict resolution skills • use appropriate technology • ensure free flow of information

tend to play by the rules of existing power structures and emphasize financial over human resources.

While members of collaborative groups led by women are more likely to maintain positive interpersonal relationships, they can experience difficulties during the implementation stage due to a lack of power and command over resources. On the other hand, collaborative ventures led by men are more likely to break down in the formative stages due to difficulties in sharing power and agreeing on a mutually beneficial agenda.

Designing an Effective Collaborative Process

THE ESSENTIALS

Most business leaders recognize the value in building long-term relationships with stakeholders and have learned the hard way that attending to the human side of these relationships can mean the difference between success and failure.[6] Bitter experience shows that a partnership gone wrong can drain precious time and other resources as participants try to solve interpersonal and organizational problems. What can companies do to avoid problems later on?

First of all, prospective partners can look at the compatibility between their organizations. Do the organizations have similar values and management styles? Do they both, for example, have "high involvement" workplaces? How do managers relate to staff? Does communication tend to be "top down" or is there an emphasis on information sharing and joint planning? Are employee relations fractious or harmonious? Does the right hand know what the left hand is doing? Ensuring compatibility at the level of values is probably the most important factor in determining the longevity of a relationship.

What about management style and goals? One way to get a clearer picture of your prospective partner's management style and goals is to consider its developmental life-cycle stage. Younger companies will tend to have different management styles and will value different things as compared with more mature companies. Recognizing your partner organization's life-cycle stage will help to determine whether your management styles and goals are likely to be complementary or conflicting.

Once a collaborative partnership has been formed, participants must effectively manage the relationships with their parent organizations in order to continue receiving their support and the necessary resources to continue the partnership. This becomes more difficult as the group develops its own identity, goals, and values that may be at odds with one or both of the parent organizations.

For relationships to grow and evolve from short-term, project-based alliances to long-term, integrated, interdependent "third way" partnerships, each party must have benefitted from the relationship in ways that are balanced over time. The group must establish a balance between action and reflection—action to test the relationship and reflection to learn from the experience and to build mutual understanding.

The partners must have developed and clarified their expectations early in the relationship and established milestones so they could evaluate the group's progress. Each partner of the group must also have been willing to learn from the others and have developed the skills to communicate effectively. Power issues must have been sorted out, and the group must have developed effective strategies for resolving conflict.

Finally, groups must develop trust. Trust is an outcome of effective, respectful communication, a history of "fair play" between members of the group, and a process of building mutual understanding and respect. Trust is another core condition that is necessary for groups to move toward greater interdependence and ultimately reach "collaborative mind"—the stage when a group ceases to focus on aspirations of individual members and attends to the collective will and mission of the group. Groups that have reached this stage have a common vision, shared language, rituals, and most importantly, the capacity to develop the most innovative and creative solutions.

Reaching "collaborative mind" doesn't happen after one or two meetings but requires an extended period of building mutual understanding, developing shared values and interests, and then testing out the relationship with concrete actions and projects. While many groups never reach this stage of development, it does represent a leap ahead in the group's capacity to generate ideas and solutions and to take action to realize opportunities.

Exhibit 3 summarizes the essential ingredients for a successful collaborative process.

RECOGNIZING ORGANIZATIONAL COMPATIBILITY

As Larraine Segil points out in her recent book, *Intelligent Business Alliances,* 55 percent of all strategic alliances dissolve within three to five years; the remaining 45 percent have a further life expectancy of 3.5 years.[7] As she also notes, the most popular forms of alliance are those that require limited interdependence between the partners, namely joint marketing and promotion and joint selling or distribution.

While it is true that most alliances are relatively short-lived and do not involve high levels of interdependence, the most profitable relationships are those that span many years and involve close ties both at organizational and interpersonal levels. Higher levels of integration and interdependence lead to lower costs to sustain the relationship and greater opportunities.

Exhibit 3: Essential Ingredients for a Successful Collaborative Process

- Effective leadership of the process
- Clearly articulated individual and collaborative goals
- Interim successes—establishing and meeting short-term goals and objectives
- People who get along and like each other
- Commitments that are honored
- Ground rules established and followed
- Sufficient financial and human resources are available to meet objectives.
- Parent organizations have made a long-term commitment.
- Communication is open and honest.
- Participants are equally committed to the relationship and to ensuring mutual benefit.
- Power balance and interdependencies between parties is roughly equal.
- Organizational cultures/work styles are compatible.
- Participants have the authority to make decisions.
- Participants have and use conflict resolution skills.
- No preconceived solution

How do potential partners assess their organizational compatibility? According to Segil, compatibility between two or more organizations with respect to their stage in the life cycle is one of the most important factors in determining the long-term viability of the partnership. To create effective, long-lasting collaborative relationships, Segil argues that partners need to understand what motivates their organizations and their managers and, further, what drives the organizations at a basic level.

She suggests that the prime determinant of an organization's needs and "personality" is the stage in its life cycle. Just as a person's age and stage in life will affect everything from finances to interests, values, and behavior, so a company's stage in its life cycle and its resulting "personality" will influence its interest in forming collaborative relationships, its choice of partners, and its definition of goals for the partnership.

Companies or organizations in the start-up phase will be looking for partnerships that increase revenues, such as equity investments, research and development, or joint venture bidding. Start-up companies are often small, new ventures that have minimal revenues. They tend to be risk-taking, founder-driven, and highly focused organizations. While benefiting from collaborative relationships, they often don't have the patience to wait for long-term relationships to develop. They also are intensely focused on their own goals and often don't have the time or resources to develop collaborative ventures.

Companies in the second rapid growth phase tend to be confident and aggressive but lacking in management depth. These companies are highly focused on increasing revenues. The CEO is often still directing traffic and following a strictly hierarchical chain of command. Forming a collaborative relationship with a rapidly growing company can be difficult.

Companies that have reached mid-life or the "professional" stage experience a leveling off of revenues, more stability, and predictability. They tend to focus more on systematizing their operations, planning, and building consensus. While still doing well in the marketplace, these companies have increased their depth-of-management capability and are better able to focus on partnerships. Companies at this stage of their life cycle are perhaps the easiest to form a collaborative relationship with.

Mature and consolidating companies have reached their maximum penetration into their markets and begin to gradually lose market share to the competition. These companies tend to be risk averse and complacent, with more rigid administrative structures and a preponderance of middle management. Their focus often shifts inward and they become less interested in forming collaborative alliances with others.

Mature companies tend to make decisions slowly, which can be a source of frustration for "younger" companies. Sometimes these companies, recognizing their stagnation, will form entrepreneurial teams to identify new partnership opportunities. If given adequate resources and decision-making authority, these teams can establish and maintain productive collaborative relationships.

Companies in decline are those that don't adapt and change to meet new market conditions, competitors, or other challenges. They are associated with inflexible structures, resistance to new ideas, and overplanning. They are the opposite of start-up companies. With a focus on form over substance, they tend to reject new ideas and initiatives. Obviously, trying to partner with this kind of a company may be an exercise in frustration.

Finally, Segil describes the "sustaining" company that avoids decline and eventual death with the infusion of new ideas, often by a visionary leader. Often this kind of sustaining company undergoes a profound transformation where old systems and structures are replaced and a new "culture" emerges. Such an organization will often pare down its operations to focus on its core competencies, forming partnerships with others along the way. While somewhat chaotic, partnerships with sustaining organizations can be fruitful and long-lasting.

Considering the life-stage of the partnering organizations can be a useful tool for deciding whether the organizations are likely to have compatible management styles and goals. While not the only predictor, it appears that life-stage, along with common values, is an important variable when it comes to the durability of collaborative relationships.

MAINTAINING SUPPORT OF PARENT ORGANIZATIONS

Building and maintaining the support of parent organizations is crucial to the long-term success of any collaborative relationship. This is, however, not as easy as it might appear. As a collaborative partnership evolves, tension will naturally arise as a result of the competing pressures for autonomy and accountability.[8] When individuals from different organizations form a collaborative alliance, they need enough autonomy to develop common goals and enough decision-making authority to implement the project seamlessly.

However, because joint venture activities can affect both parent organizations, the individuals also need to be accountable to the organizations they represent. So a balance must be found between ensuring autonomy and building in accountability. It is, for example, not feasible for those involved in the collaborative venture to be continually checking with the parent company for direction. Too much checking can cause inertia and result in significant time delays.

SELECTING MEMBERS OF THE COLLABORATIVE TEAM

The members of the collaborative group should also be carefully chosen with an eye to maintaining as much continuity as possible. While it is important to be aware of the tendency for groups to get "stale" and lose their creativity, continuity is important to allow interpersonal relationships time to build and trust to develop. If individuals must leave the group, transition time should be allowed to find and initiate another partner. It is also important to involve individuals who can commit resources on behalf of their organization without going back for approval, who are fully briefed on their organization's overall strategic direction, and ideally, who are known and respected by at least some members of the partnering organization.

Effective and committed champions from each of the involved organizations play a vital role in establishing and legitimizing the relationship. Their role goes beyond cheerleading and developing grass-roots support within host organizations to ensuring resources are available when needed, telling stories about the alliance, simplifying the approvals process, explaining how decisions are made, and introducing their partners to individuals in the organization who can help them.[9]

EQUALIZING THE POWER BALANCE

Equalizing a power balance between participants is critical to the success of collaborative ventures. For example, while the involvement of a senior leader in the relationship-building process can be extremely valuable, that person needs to come to the table as an equal member of the group, leaving power and status differentials at the door. A collaborative process depends on all participants feeling that their contributions will be valued and that they will be treated with respect and consideration.

When an imbalance exists, it is important for the partners to discuss who will contribute what and to come up with a plan to ensure that the contributions are fair and equitable. Participants must come to accept the legitimacy of each other's role and contributions, acknowledge their interdependence, and make a real commitment to partnership.

Allowing time in the process to talk about who is bringing what expertise to the table can shift the dynamics toward a more equal partnership. Partners are also more likely to share power equally if they are to some extent dependent on each other. Increasing interdependence occurs with time as individuals begin to trust one another and accept the vulnerability that comes with interdependence.

BUILDING TRUST

For collaboration to work, trusting relationships must be developed between individuals and, over time, between organizations. The conditions that give rise to trust and the nature of trust remain constant in relationships between organizations or relationships between individuals.

WHAT IS TRUST?

Social scientists and philosophers have long argued that trust is essential for stable social relationships because it promotes cooperation and with it the potential for mutual benefit. Trust has been defined by University of Michigan professor LaRue Hosmer as "the reliance by one person, group, or firm upon a voluntarily accepted duty on the part of another person, group, or firm to recognize and protect the rights and interests of all others engaged in a joint endeavor or economic exchange."[10]

In simpler terms, trust is the expectation that others will behave honorably and that there will be a mix of give and take in the relationship. In trusting relationships, both partners have each other's best interests at heart and therefore they are willing to both relinquish some of their independence and increase their level of interdependence.

Trust is rarely all encompassing; people often trust others only to do certain things. For example, I trust my mechanic to keep my car in good running order, but I wouldn't trust him to look after my children. Similarly, an organization might trust one supplier but not another to source and consolidate materials for a manufacturing process, depending on its experience and track record.

Trusting relationships are based on an expectation of fair play. An individual assesses the "fairness" of his or her relationship with another party based on two different criteria—distributive justice, or how big a piece of the pie each person gets, and procedural justice, or the perceived fairness of the relationship-building process.

While both are important, procedural justice concerns have the greatest impact on trust. Ensuring that partners see the relationship-building process as fair and equitable by enhancing procedural justice is often more powerful in establishing trust than dealing at great length with issues related to distributive justice. This is because individuals believe their partners can more easily control *how* they relate to them but perhaps not how resources are shared.

BENEFITS OF TRUST

As we noted in earlier sections of the book, trusting relationships between an organization and its stakeholders can be a source of competitive advantage. Trusting relationships can have significant bottom-line benefits for companies. As Nirmalya Kumar points out in a *Harvard Business Review* article on the power of trust in manufacturer-retailer relationships, retailers with trusting relationships with manufacturers generated more sales and therefore more profits for both the retailer and manufacturer.[11] His research showed that retailers with "high trust" relationships generated 78 percent more sales than those with "low trust" relationships. This is because trust encourages information sharing, innovation, better pricing, and lower monitoring costs.

By the same token, when a company uses its power unethically to influence the behavior of stakeholders such as suppliers or citizens, it may experience bottom-line benefits in the short term, but these practices will be self-defeating in the longer term. Kumar points out that when companies systematically exploit their advantage, those that are negatively affected inevitably fight back.

While the level of trust that exists between a company and stakeholder organizations can be influenced by policies, procedures, and more formal agreements or contracts, trust inevitably comes down to the quality of interpersonal relationships. While legal contracts, rules, and other controls are often needed at the beginning of a relationship, these kinds of coercive measures often become less important in longer relationships. In fact, formal legal contracts have been found to reduce innovation and cooperative behaviors in established groups.

Trust develops over time as interpersonal relationships between members of a group are strengthened and the group develops a history of shared success and fair dealing. As members become more trusting and more committed to the group, they will come to rely less on formal legal contracts and more on implicit psychological contracts. They will be informal and flexible and not based on formalized contracts but rather on ethical behavior, mutual opportunities, and obligations.

Companies can forge stronger, more trusting relationships with a few rather than a large number of stakeholder groups. Establishing and maintaining links with a few key stakeholders means that there will be more resources to devote to each relationship and more opportunities to exploit.

Case Study: Long-Term Relationships with Suppliers

One of the most well-known retail chains, Marks & Spencer, puts a lot of effort into building trusting relationships with its suppliers.[12] The company establishes long-term partnerships with suppliers by

- refusing to accept prices that are too low to enable the suppliers to reinvest and improve their products
- helping manufacturers re-engineer products to reduce costs
- ensuring open and honest dialogue, even encouraging criticism of company practices
- providing suppliers with access cards to enter corporate head offices
- arranging trips with suppliers to trade shows and to visit foreign suppliers of raw materials
- taking time to explain policies and actions to suppliers
- explaining its vision and strategies
- visiting manufacturers' sites to gain an appreciation of their local conditions

DEALING WITH CONFLICT

To be successful in the long term, collaborative partners must find third-way solutions to conflicts. Creating integrative solutions provides an alternative to domination or compromise. As management theorist Mary Follett recognized over fifty years ago, domination is not usually successful in the long run because the side that is defeated will simply wait for its chance to dominate. Similarly, with compromise, neither side gets what it wants, and hence the conflict will occur again and again in some other form.

The tension generated by differences can be the source of creative ideas that add value to the partnership. Allowing and encouraging a process of constructive conflict and respectful debate can result in a more productive, creative group process. This process of integration forces the group to define itself and its common purpose. It can make all the difference between groups that reach "collaborative mind" and those that burn out slowly or rise like a shining star and burn out quickly.

While groups need to develop strategies and procedures for managing conflict in the early stages, the ongoing, sometimes time-consuming and difficult struggle to define common ground is extremely important in the long term. As Mary Follett wrote, "The common idea and the common will are born together in the social process."

Since conflict resolution is a large, well-established discipline, groups and individuals will find many excellent books, workshops, and videos available to help them develop the necessary skills to handle conflict productively.

COMMUNICATION

SETTING GROUND RULES

Respectful communication also depends on setting ground rules early in the process that are accepted and followed by all members. Establishing ground rules to ensure respectful interpersonal communication helps create a "safe" environment within which individuals feel free to express their views, without fear of "looking stupid," being criticized, or otherwise sanctioned. Respectful communication can cover a range of verbal as well as nonverbal actions. Often it is the details that matter.

Groups should establish the ground rules for communication and conflict resolution before problems arise so that members will feel free to engage in debate and so that problems will be dealt with immediately and not left to fester or be ignored altogether. People must be comfortable raising issues and problems before they turn into major conflicts and must have the confidence that they will be treated respectfully without personal attack. They must each develop superb negotiating skills in order to ensure their interests are met in the long term.

EMPHASIZING COOPERATION AND INTEGRATION

A collaborative partnership must also nurture a spirit of inquiry so that participants are rewarded for exploration and innovation, not for selling their own preconceived ideas or solutions. Conflict will be reduced dramatically if the group defines itself in cooperative as opposed to competitive terms. Clarifying expectations, values, and assumptions and acknowledging the value of each partner's contribution will help to foster cooperation. Dialogue allows for better decisions and renewed sense of ownership. (See chapter 6 for a fuller discussion of the dialogue method.)

The group also must identify situations where integrative solutions aren't feasible. While these situations are more infrequent than we may believe, there is no point trying to create a win-win solution when the situation unequivocally has winners and losers.

SELECTING PARTNERS WITH GOOD COMMUNICATION SKILLS

Ideal partners are those with excellent communication and conflict resolution skills who are philosophically committed to cooperation and collaboration. To create an environment within which open and honest dialogue can occur, partners should be chosen carefully with consideration of their personality, values, and skills.

Partners often spend a great deal of time resolving interpersonal issues caused by poor communication skills. Inflexible people can impede discussion. If they haven't developed good communication skills or attempt to control the discussion, progress will be hampered and other participants will be discouraged from speaking. Consider encouraging the group to invest in training if necessary and to spend time developing and agreeing on ground rules for discussions.

COMMUNICATION SYSTEMS AND PROTOCOLS

Participants also need to have equal access to information. Information systems technology can help to make the information accessible and useful, but the partners must also have the will and resources to permit information sharing. The following are some of the questions partners can discuss to ensure that the appropriate communication protocols and systems are in place.

- How frequently should we communicate?
- Who will communicate with whom?
- What communication channels are most appropriate?
- What types of information will be shared?
- What information is proprietary?
- How will we deal with communication problems?
- What aspect of our respective corporate cultures might hinder communication?
- How can we overcome those barriers?

THE SETTING

Time spent meeting face-to-face is essential for a collaborative group to establish itself as a unified whole. While it is possible to use computer technology and other communication aids to increase the effectiveness of information sharing and planning, there is no substitute for meeting together. Communication experts suggest that this is because face-to-face dialogue increases exposure to all cues, especially nonverbal ones.

Getting out of the meeting room and into a more informal environment can also evoke more personal and emotional conversations, enabling people to realize they have more in common than they might have thought.

People work best together when they appreciate other points of view and can move past biased preconceptions. Especially in the early stages of building a relationship, partners need to have opportunities to show others how and where they carry out their work—in the laboratory, the retail store, or the community.

Case Study: Listening and Communicating Effectively

British Telecommunications (BT), the country's largest telecommunications company, has instituted an innovative set of processes for listening to stakeholders in order to "anticipate concerns, identify best practices and avoid stakeholder disaffection in the marketplace."[13] These initiatives also help to foster dialogue between stakeholder groups and BT and, in the long run, to cement the relationships with those groups. Following are some of the key mechanisms BT uses for listening and responding to stakeholders:

- *Liaison Panels:* Representative groups of residential and small business customers meet with BT managers to solve problems and discuss new ideas. The panels stimulate BT to answer questions it might not otherwise ask and provide feedback it needs but may not want to hear.

There are two types of panels. General panels address any and all issues, and single-issue panels focus on specific topics. Both types deal with issues ranging from image and reputation to indebtedness and advertising policy. Panel members are not a statistically valid sample but are chosen to represent various stakeholder interests. BT's environmental panel, for example, includes local residents, BT managers, professional environmentalists, local business owners, researchers and academics, and high school students.

- *Stakeholder Forums:* BT sponsors these one-day events to bring a mix of community leaders together to discuss issues such as privacy, corporate integrity, or legislation dealing with employee issues. Besides stimulating open discussion, the forums also foster collaborative action between the participants. Topics for the forums come from external groups, the liaison panels, or from within BT.

The forums reflect BT's concern with broader social issues and help the company develop wider networks with community stakeholders. They also provide an opportunity for BT to get involved in collaborative ventures with other stakeholders to address issues that affect BT in the long run but are not directly related to its operations.

- *Issues Exchanges:* BT sponsors working groups to address trends and complex issues with national or global implications. The conclusions reached by the working groups are brought to the attention of government policymakers. The issue exchanges give BT an opportunity to build positive relationships with scientists and other experts as well as government regulators.

Input from these different processes is collected, analyzed, and presented by BT's chief executive to the Board Executive Committee every six months. Issues requiring action are debated and resolved by the Issues Steering Group, which is chaired by the Director of Corporate Relations with members from major divisions. In this way, BT ensures that the feedback from stakeholders is used, and thus they will be willing to participate in future initiatives.

COMMUNICATING IN HIGH-STAKES–LOW-TRUST SITUATIONS

Communication can be particularly challenging in low-trust, high-stakes situations. In these situations, individuals' behavior will be shaped by their perceptions. If they don't trust others in the group, if they don't feel they have control over decisions that will be made by the group, and if they believe they could be negatively affected by the decision, they will be unable to process information. In low-trust situations, people also become highly selective about what sources of information they choose to receive and which information they believe. Cognitive static or mental noise will interrupt their ability to hear what others are saying and communicate their own feelings accurately.

Opposition by community groups and citizens to corporate plans and projects is often related to short- and long-term problems with communication. In the short term, companies don't communicate early enough and with adequate attention paid to the interests and concerns of the stakeholders. In the long term, the company must establish credibility and develop a sense of reciprocity with the community. Research shows that the most important factor in earning the trust of the stakeholders is to demonstrate caring and concern for the issues that are personally important to them.

Social Accounting—An Essential Management Tool

In the successful firms, the magic is not in what they do, it is in what they are and what they stand for.

—J. Liedtka, M. Haskins, J. Rosenblum, and J. Weber, 1997

This chapter focuses on social accounting—the practice of systematically recording, presenting, and interpreting a company's nonfinancial or "social" accounts. Social accounting provides a framework for companies to assess the effectiveness of their relationship-building efforts and also to improve the quality and resilience of those relationships.

In this chapter we provide an overview of current social accounting practices, their relevance for relationship-building, and some of the challenges and limitations of each method. We then describe a new management-oriented approach to social accounting. This new approach differs from existing social accounting methods because it integrates accounting processes with strategy development, budgeting, and other decision-making cycles. It also is designed to provide decision-relevant information to help managers and employees improve stakeholder relationships and business processes. This new approach stresses feedback and learning.

A management-oriented approach also not emphasize verification of audit results by external auditors. It starts from a less adversarial position because the accounting process is seen as part of an ongoing relationship-building initiative. It is assumed that companies will engage in dialogue with their stakeholders and that corporate strategies will be aligned with stakeholder expectations. In this context, the collection and publication of nonfinancial performance information, including feedback from stakeholders, simply formalizes, regularizes, and integrates existing two-way communication processes.

While social accounting can be practiced by companies that have not adopted a collaborative approach to stakeholder relations, measuring corporate impact beyond the financial bottom line and incorporating that information into decision-making and management systems is essential if companies are going to build a network of mutually beneficial relationships.

The following table summarizes the main steps involved in evaluating and improving stakeholder relationships. We will be covering them in this chapter and the next.

Table 12
Evaluation of Relationships

Tasks	Tools/Method	Results
• design and conduct stakeholder audit • celebrate successes • learn from failures	• stakeholder audit	• impact of relationship building on corporation measured • regular communication channel with stakeholders established • values aligned between stakeholders and the corporation

Review of Social Accounting Methods

Social accounting is still in its infancy, with many companies trying and refining various approaches as they search for ways to realize the full potential of this assessment tool. To date, North American companies are not legally required to produce social accounts. Audits are voluntary and unregulated—although more and more companies are undertaking some form of social accounting.

Companies as diverse as Ben and Jerry's Homemade, IKEA, British Telecom, KLM Airlines, The Body Shop, and VanCity Credit Union have prepared various forms of social accounts in the past several years. These accounts, which have received considerable public and media attention, have varied considerably in scope and methodology.

EARLY SOCIAL ACCOUNTING

While academics have been interested in social accounting for several decades, there has been a lack of generally accepted methodology and measurement techniques. The term "social audit" was first used in the 1940s and 1950s in the debate about corporate social responsibility. The practice of social auditing expanded in the early 1970s with attempts by academics to measure the social effects of corporate behavior. These early audits focused on reporting corporate social expenditures and eventually bogged down in methodological and measurement issues, particularly the problem of how to establish the social costs and benefits of corporate actions. The recession in the late 1970s meant less attention was paid to corporate social responsibility issues in general.

ETHICAL SCREENING

In the mid-1980s, interest in a form of social reporting known as "ethical screening" surged, as several firms in North America and Europe began collecting and publishing corporate social-performance profiles. Companies such as Social Audit Ltd., based in the United States, promoted the idea that companies should be required to disclose information about their social impacts, not just their financial dealings. This led to the current practice of companies such as Kinder, Lydenberg, Domini and Co. in the United States and the Social Investment Organization in Canada, who use social responsibility criteria to screen companies, primarily for the ethical investment market.

SOCIAL REPORTS

Ben and Jerry's began publishing an assessment of its company's social performance in its 1988 annual report—earlier than any other company in North America. These reports were initially designed as a tool for management to ensure that the company was achieving its social mission and goals. They were prepared by an external researcher based on interviews with staff and other stockholders and a review of company policies and procedures. The reports commented on issues such as recycling and other environmental initiatives, workplace safety, employee satisfaction, corporate philanthropy, and pay equity for men and women.

CONTEMPORARY SOCIAL AUDITS

The New Economics Foundation (NEF), a British nonprofit organization, has spearheaded the development of a new, more systematic and rigorous approach to social auditing. NEF defines a social audit as a tool for assessing, reporting on, and ultimately enhancing an organization's relationships with its stakeholders.

Compared with social reports, the NEF social audit methodology is more quantitative, comprehensive, and oriented toward the verification of corporate social responsibility claims. NEF assumes the role of an external auditor and also forms an independent audit review panel to further verify the quality and independence of its work. Within an NEF social audit process, external stakeholders play a major role in identifying performance indicators. These audits have emphasized verification rather than management concerns.

The following table gives some examples of the various aspects of corporate performance that are assessed in an NEF social audit.

Table 13
Items Assessed in a Social Audit

Commitments	Response Process	Policies & Programs	Outcomes
Corporate philanthropy goals	• decisions by donations committee • staff volunteer activities	• funding criteria • paid time off for staff volunteering	• amount of money donated • hours volunteered
Environmental sustainability principles	• environmental management process	• environmental policy • recycling program	• tons of solid waste going to landfill
Code of ethics	• monitoring and compliance process	• policies governing gifts • ethics training	• number of ethics complaints
Commitment to open communication with stakeholders	• intranet system • regular "brown bag" sessions with staff	• teleconferences • bottom-up evaluations	• performance records disclosed in an audit report
Commitment to participation	• participative decision-making process	• employee profit-sharing plan	• annual dividends received by staff

Case Study: The Evolution of Social Auditing

In 1991, Traidcraft plc, a "fair-trading" organization based in Britain, decided to conduct a social audit. Traidcraft was founded in the early 1980s to develop fair trade with the Third World based on Christian principles of concern for others and social justice. Traidcraft directors were looking for ways to bring noneconomic criteria such as social justice and environmental sustainability into their own corporate decision-making processes, especially with respect to the company's international operations. Traidcraft has been one of the proponents and developers of the contemporary version of social auditing over the past decade.

The Body Shop's first social audit, designed and conducted with the help of the New Economics Foundation and published as part of its *1995 International Values Report,* is one of the most extensive and expensive social audits ever conducted. Its social audit, separate from the environmental audit and animal protection assessment, focused on how UK-based employees, suppliers, community grant recipients, customers, and shareholders perceived the company's performance. Focus groups, surveys, and interviews were used to collect opinions from these stakeholders. Managers identified performance standards based on industry "best practices" and collected quantitative data over the course of a year. Statistics such as staff community-volunteering rates and foundation donations were used to measure The Body Shop's community involvement relative to other international corporations. Staff turnover and salary differentials were used as performance indicators in the human resources area, and dividends and share price performance were used to assess performance related to shareholders.

The widely distributed social audit report included a description of the research methodology, a statement by company founders, an overview of major company policies and programs related to each stakeholder group, a summary of feedback from each group, and statistics related to key performance areas. Successes and problem areas were also highlighted, along with a statement by management about how The Body Shop aimed to address problem areas. As is the case with a financial audit, the social auditors provided a statement verifying the accuracy of the results. A thirteen-member audit advisory panel of experts chosen by NEF assessed the audit process and results.

ETHICAL ACCOUNTING

Meanwhile, Peter Pruzan, a professor of systems science at the Copenhagen Business School, has developed a different approach to social accounting—ethical accounting. Ethical accounting brings the views of stakeholders into the management arena via an extended process of dialogue. Although talked about in the same breath as social auditing, ethical accounting's focus has not been on objectively assessing and reporting corporate social performance but rather creating an alignment between corporate and stakeholder values. Stakeholders even make recommendations for changes to corporate policies and programs and review and comment on company budgets.

Ethical accounting was pioneered by Sbn Bank in Denmark. Since 1990, more than fifty companies in Denmark have gone through an ethical accounting process. Each company identifies shared core values through a series of "conversations" with employees, customers, shareholders, and local community representatives. It then drafts value statements and turns them into a survey questionnaire for members of key stakeholder groups. The results of the survey—the ethical accounting statement—provide a company and its stakeholders with a measure of how well the company has lived up to its social values.

from Public Relations to Value Alignment: Different Methods for Different Purposes

Social accounting methods have developed in order to serve specific purposes. Social audits have been primarily used to report on and verify the claims a company makes about its social performance. Ethical accounting, on the other hand, serves as a mechanism for companies to listen to and respond more effectively to stakeholders. Though less common, a few companies have experimented with management-oriented accounting procedures. While most audits reflect a combination of purposes and methodologies, the following description of three social accounting approaches is provided for illustrative purposes.

SOCIAL AUDITS: VERIFICATION OF CLAIMS

Many of the higher-profile social audits conducted recently—such as that of The Body Shop and Ben and Jerry's Homemade, Inc.—have been primarily used to report on and verify claims regarding the impact of corporate activities on stakeholders and the natural environment. As the nonfinancial impacts of corporate actions are more closely scrutinized, from concerns about pollution to the impact of company initiatives on nearby residents and communities, public and investor pressure for this kind of corporate accountability intensifies.

A "public relations" audit provides a verifiable source of information to back up a company's claims—information that can help develop public and stakeholder trust and may lead to greater sales, investor confidence, and other benefits.

ETHICAL ACCOUNTING FOR VALUE ALIGNMENT

Some companies are using ethical accounting to listen to customers, employees, suppliers, community organizations, and other stakeholders in order to understand how corporate actions affect them and how they perceive the company and its operations. Ethical accounting provides a more formal opportunity for a company to demonstrate its commitment to sharing information, consulting strategic partners, and involving stakeholders in decisions that affect them—all important elements of building trusting relationships.

Through this type of social accounting process, stakeholders become more familiar with corporate values and ethics that affect them. The process gives stakeholders a structured voice and through a process of dialogue provides the company with valuable clues about risk management.

MANAGEMENT-ORIENTED SOCIAL ACCOUNTING

Academics, some large accounting firms, and several leading-edge companies are experimenting with various social accounting methods that are oriented to improving a company's bottom-line performance by helping firms manage "intangible" assets such as ethical performance and reputation.

Management-oriented approaches are being spurred by the interests and needs of both boards of directors and senior managers. Progressive

---

Exhibit 4. Sample questions from Sbn's 1993
Ethical Accounting Statement
(Numbers are percentages)

A. EMPLOYEES

1. You are proud to work at Sbn Bank.

Strongly agree	60
Slightly agree	30
Slightly disagree	4
Strongly disagree	1
No opinion	5

2. You believe your job is meaningful.

Strongly agree	78
Slightly agree	19
Slightly disagree	2
Strongly disagree	0
No opinion	1

B. CUSTOMERS

1. Sbn Bank advises against investments that, in its opinion, are too risky.

Strongly agree	29
Slightly agree	8
Slightly disagree	5
Strongly disagree	6
No opinion	52

2. The local community trusts Sbn Bank.

Strongly agree	57
Slightly agree	22
Slightly disagree	4
Strongly disagree	3
No opinion	14

Source: P. Pruzan, "The Ethical Dimensions of Banking: Sbn Bank, Denmark," in *Building Corporate Accountability: Emerging Practices in Social and Ethical Accounting, Auditing and Reporting*, ed. S. Zadek, P. Pruzan, R. Evans. (London: Earthscan Publications Ltd., 1997).

---

boards, for example, are asking for access to data on environmental management, employee relations, and joint venture arrangements to ensure the company's actions are ethical and within legal bounds and to be better able to provide good strategic advice. Managers want to be able to measure the impact of corporate strategies on employee learning and growth and customer satisfaction because they recognize that those variables drive financial performance.

Management-oriented approaches to social accounting are in a developmental stage and range from the cost-benefit approach used by the consulting firm SmithO'Brien in Boston to KPMG's ethical auditing service.

The following table summarizes these three different approaches to social accounting, their priority audiences, main purposes, methodological features, and foci of attention.

Table 14
Summary of Social Accounting Approaches

Focus of Audit	Priority Audiences	Main Purpose	Methodological Features	Focus of Attention
Public relations	investors consumers media	verification of social performance claims	independent auditor, validation of indicators, social record keeping	stakeholder perceptions direct impacts on stakeholders
Value Alignment	stakeholders management	mutual understanding between stakeholders and company	dialogue with stakeholders, values statement based on questionnaire	stakeholder perceptions, alignment in values
Management	executives boards of directors	continuous improvement of performance, management of "intangible" assets	mix of quantitative and qualitative measures	secondary drivers of financial performance, integration of results into management systems

Problems with Social Accounting

COST

The cost of conducting an audit or ethical accounting process can range from several thousand dollars for a cursory audit of a small company to several hundred thousand for a full audit with stakeholder dialogue, depending on the size of the organization, the scope of the audit, the involvement of outside consultants and auditors, and employees' level of participation. The number of person-days needed to conduct a social audit of a medium-size firm ranges from about 10 to 120.

POTENTIAL CRITICISM IN THE MEDIA AND BY STAKEHOLDERS

Companies complain that social audits are not only very expensive but also can expose them to unwanted negative media coverage and criticism from stakeholder groups. Undertaking social accounting and disclosing the results carries real risks. Companies that retain independent auditors may end up seeing negative aspects of their operations make headlines. Positive results may also unrealistically raise expectations on the part of staff members, consumers, and the general public.

LACK OF STANDARD METHODOLOGY

While lauded by some for bringing information about nonfinancial aspects of corporate performance into the public domain, others criticize social reports because they are based on researchers' subjective impressions and lack external verification of the conclusions reached. Social audits, like the one prepared by The Body Shop, are sometimes criticized for being no more than a thinly disguised public relations tool that uses numbers, market research, and supposedly independent researchers to create the impression of rigor and objectivity.

Controversy also rages about the use of quantitative and qualitative measures. Some argue that hard data (usually financial) is essential to enable businesses to make sense of the social impacts of their activities. Others suggest that in many cases, social effects cannot be measured through traditional quantitative measures.

MEASUREMENT DIFFICULTIES

Social accounting has been plagued by disagreements over measurement. Compared to the relatively straightforward process of measuring the impact of economic transactions, isolating and measuring intangible social impacts is a highly subjective process. For example, common sense tells us that a company's sponsorship of community events through financial grants, in-kind donations, and/or employee volunteer support can make a community more vibrant and cohesive, contributing to an enhanced quality of life for residents in the long term. However, measuring community cohesion and establishing a link between company activities and changes in quality of life is imprecise at best.

In addition, attaching monetary value to the direct impacts of corporate actions—on public health and the environment, for example—is difficult because the costs are shared by many and may not necessarily be known immediately. Placing value on externalities is a subjective process and is as difficult as measuring quality of life.

Recent developments in accounting and evaluation research also suggest that assessing the value of intangible assets, such as customer satisfaction or employee learning and growth, means stepping back and measuring performance on the drivers of those outcomes. This kind of performance measurement is more complex and may involve repeated rounds of data collection to glean the importance of various factors. It also involves direct observation and solicitation of feedback from stakeholders.

LACK OF INTEGRATION INTO MANAGEMENT SYSTEMS

Finally, both community stakeholders and corporate decision makers have decried the lack of effective mechanisms for integrating social-audit results into corporate decision-making systems, thereby limiting their utility for driving actual improvements in social performance. This may be because social accounting has generally been carried out by social activists and academics to put pressure on corporations to be more socially responsible. But circumstances are changing. Companies are beginning to express an interest in using social accounting as a management tool.

A New Management-Oriented Approach to Social Accounting

The word audit comes from the Latin word *audire*, "to listen or hear." While many of the current accounting methods, like social audits and ethical accounting, do a good job of listening to stakeholders, they fall short in terms of helping companies monitor and improve their overall performance and especially their stakeholder relationships. Given the relative newness of the social accounting field and the fact that most approaches have been geared toward ensuring corporate accountability, the lack of sophisticated management processes is to be expected.

A new management-oriented approach to social accounting is needed to provide information that companies can use to monitor and improve their stakeholder relationships. Such a system would support corporate strategy development, the continuous improvement of business processes and relationships, and the building of trust through greater accountability. It would

- bring essential information about the interests, perspectives, and expectations of stakeholders into the strategy development process
- provide companies with the information they need to effectively monitor and manage implicit and explicit stakeholder contracts
- ensure that corporate goals for each stakeholder group are clearly understood and translated into action at all levels of the organization

- help to build the trust of all stakeholders by making information available about the company's broad impacts on society

The following is a description of the main elements of a management-oriented social accounting approach. The details of how to design and implement such a social accounting system is covered in the next chapter.

ACCOUNTING PROCESS LINKED TO STRATEGY DEVELOPMENT

A management-oriented approach to social accounting links stakeholder dialogue with strategy development. It includes mechanisms by which companies can systematically gather information about what stakeholders expect and need from the corporation and simultaneously communicate company goals and intentions. This two-way communication process is essential if companies are to develop strategies that are aligned with the expectations of their stakeholders. As we discussed in the context of the model of corporate-stakeholder relations presented in chapter 3, companies must meet their stakeholder's expectations in order to maintain the contract-based relationship.

Customers, for example, will not buy products that fail to meet price, quality, and service requirements. Communities will not tolerate companies that fail to meet legal obligations and social expectations. If employees' expectations about what they will receive from the company for their contributions are not met, they will be less motivated to develop the skills and knowledge that are essential for innovation. Companies must understand what their stakeholders want and need and then use that information to design strategies that will enable them to meet those expectations.

SOCIAL ACCOUNTING SYSTEM PROVIDES DECISION-RELEVANT INFORMATION

Traditional financial measurement systems—and even social audits—are not designed to communicate decision-relevant information to people inside a corporation. As a recent Conference Board of Canada report notes, financial measures are excessively historical, they lack predictive power, reward the wrong behavior, do not capture important changes until it's too late, and give too little consideration to intangible assets such as social and intellectual capital.[2] Social audits, on the other hand, typically focus on outcomes of corporate activity that are important to external stakeholders rather than managers.

A management-oriented social accounting system provides companies with information they need to continuously improve their social performance. The measurement system focuses on the increasingly important intangible drivers of long-term financial success such as employee know-how, supplier trust and commitment, customer satisfaction, and corporate reputation.

This kind of information can help managers decide how and when to make investments in relationships with employees, customers, suppliers, and communities, actions that ultimately create value and competitive advantage. By investing in employee learning, for example, companies can build intellectual capital. Similarly, fostering trusting relationships with suppliers can reduce costs of monitoring and managing formal contracts.

ENSURING HORIZONTAL CONSISTENCY AND VERTICAL COORDINATION

A management-oriented approach to social accounting helps to improve social performance by ensuring that stakeholder goals and strategies are acted on consistently across all parts of the organization. For this to occur, employees and managers must be aware of and motivated to make the necessary changes to their behavior. Employee involvement in setting targets and milestones is critical to creating a sense of ownership and commitment to both the broad strategic goals and the audit.

The system is also designed to foster vertical coordination by making employees and managers aware of strategic goals for each stakeholder group and then ensuring that the goals are translated into individual and business unit objectives.

Clear measurable goals, objectives, and performance indicators for each stakeholder group are established as part of the process of building the accounting system. Based on those goals, performance objectives are clearly laid out for each department and team so that all employees understand how their actions contribute to reaching performance targets. In this way, employees' performance can also be evaluated according to how well they achieve corporate and team social goals, a process that will create both momentum and accountability.

INCORPORATING SOCIAL ACCOUNTING RESULTS INTO
DECISION-MAKING PROCEDURES

Management-oriented social accounting draws a stronger connection among social accounting and strategic planning, budgeting, and other decision-making processes. This ensures that the company's spending and actions support its stakeholder goals as well as financial goals. For example, social accounting information is systematically fed into a strategic planning/budgeting cycle so that companies can fund initiatives that will enable them to achieve their long-term social goals as well as short-term financial targets.

Also, internal systems and structures are aligned to remove barriers and provide the necessary support for improving corporate social performance. For example, an audit may show that performance evaluations and compensation programs need to be revamped to reward employees for meeting team and departmental social as well as sales objectives. The company's internal communication system may need to be redesigned to ensure that information critical to job satisfaction is accessible to employees. Or to increase public trust, the company's external relations program may need to be extended to include opportunities for dialogue between community stakeholders and senior managers. This stage of aligning internal systems and structures based on social accounting results is a vital stage in the improvement process.

RELATIONSHIP BUILDING INSTEAD OF VERIFICATION

Finally, a management-oriented approach focuses less attention on verification and more on the process of relationship building. By collecting and disclosing social accounting information, companies build the trust of their stakeholders and in so doing strengthen their relationships. Stakeholders can assess whether companies have fulfilled their side of the contractual relationship and whether, overall, the company has lived up to its core values and its claims. Through a process of measuring, reporting, and seeking feedback on its nonfinancial impacts, the company serves its own interests as well as the interests of its stakeholders and society.

Therefore, though companies may decide to undertake social accounting for ethical reasons or to verify their claims, taken from the perspective of a collaborative model of corporate-stakeholder relations, social accounting is a vital element of building stronger stakeholder relationships and ultimately improving a company's financial and social performance.

In the next chapter, we will outline the steps to designing and implementing a stakeholder audit within a strategic management system.

Stakeholder Audit: A Tool for Assessing and Improving Stakeholder Relationships

In the networked world, everything about a company can be known: every slipup, policy and practice . . . The world can easily see organizations for what they are, not what they pretend to be.

—Esther Dyson, 1997

This chapter provides a step-by-step guide to designing and implementing a stakeholder audit. The audit process is part of a strategic management system in that it is linked to strategy development, budgeting, and other decision-making activities. The stakeholder audit is also designed to support the feedback and learning that is so crucial for relationship-building. It provides opportunities for stakeholder dialogue as well the collection and analysis of "hard" information about the impacts of corporate activities on various stakeholder groups. Finally, the production and dissemination of the audit report beyond the walls of the corporation helps to build trust by ensuring accountability.

The guide to conducting a fully integrated stakeholder audit is based on the following key points:

- Corporate social performance refers to the effect that a company has on all of its stakeholders through direct and indirect relationships.

- Most companies should begin with a relatively simple baseline stakeholder audit the first year and progress to a more comprehensive audit with broader stakeholder involvement in subsequent audit cycles.

- A stakeholder audit should ultimately measure performance in six areas: employee well-being, learning and growth, customer satisfaction and values, reputation and relationships with communities and suppliers, environmental sustainability, and fiscal and social accountability.

- Measures of corporate social performance should be explicitly linked to corporate strategic goals for each stakeholder group.

- Employees should be involved in developing individual and team social performance/relationship-building objectives and targets to ensure that the targets are realistic and employees are motivated to achieve them.

- Dialogue with external stakeholders should be ongoing.

- The results of the audit should be incorporated into decision-making systems so that corporate social performance and stakeholder relationships can be continuously improved.

While designing and conducting a stakeholder audit can be time-consuming and can be complicated by methodological questions, the following step-by-step guide should eliminate many of the problems associated with this process and keep the audit process effective and productive.

Exhibit 5 describes the steps that need to be taken to design and implement a stakeholder audit and to integrate the results into a strategic management system. Because the first three steps are discussed in earlier chapters of the book, they will not be dealt with at length here.

Case Study: The VanCity Credit Union Experience

Though still being practiced in their unique forms, the three approaches are converging. VanCity Credit Union is perhaps the

Exhibit 5: Framework for a Fully Integrated Stakeholder Audit

Step 1. Define the purpose and scope of the audit

- Why do we want to monitor social performance?
- How important to us is improving social performance?
- Is senior management committed?
- How will results of the audit be used?
- Who are our stakeholders and which ones will be involved in the audit?
- Do we have an audit implementation plan?

Step 2. Clarify social mission, values and goals

- What is important to us beyond financial performance?
- What values define our company?
- What are our stakeholder goals?
- How are our stakeholder goals linked to financial goals and our overall business strategy?
- Have our employees been involved in developing the social mission, values, and goals?
- Do they understand and support the mission and goals?

Step 3. Perform baseline assessment and gap analysis

- What management systems affect our organization's social performance?
- What policies govern various aspects of our social performance?
- What practices define our company's current social performance?
- What are "best practices" related to our business?
- What are our stakeholders' expectations of us? How satisfied are they with the relationship?
- What are our social performance strengths and weaknesses?
- What are the major gaps and liabilities?
- How can they be addressed?

Step 4. Develop social performance measures

- Do our stakeholder goals need to be refined based on baseline-assessment results and stakeholder dialogue?
- What are the key drivers or factors that will influence our success in meeting stakeholder goals?
- What strategies will help us meet our social goals?
- What indicators can be used to measure progress?   *continues...*

- Do managers responsible for implementing corporate strategies agree with this analysis?
- What do key stakeholders think about the indicators and targets?

Step 5. Design a social performance monitoring system
- What data are we already collecting?
- Where are the gaps?
- What additional information needs to be collected?
- How will it be collected?
- By whom?
- How often?

Step 6. Prepare a stakeholder audit report
- Have all the data been compiled? Are they accurate and complete?
- What do they tell us about our social performance in specific areas?
- What are our strengths and weaknesses?
- Where do we need to improve?
- How should this information be summarized?
- How should it be communicated to stakeholders?

Step 7. Review results with stakeholders
- What process or tools should we use to solicit feedback (e.g. surveys, focus groups, interviews)?
- How should the feedback be synthesized?
- What does the feedback tell us about our social performance?
- How do we need to revise our corporate goals and strategies?
- Do we have the right indicators?
- What targets should be set for next year?

Step 8. Align corporate systems and structures
- What internal changes are needed to improve social performance?
- Are there linkages between our corporate strategies and divisional and individual performance objectives and targets?
- Do our reward and recognition programs support employees in their efforts to improve social performance?
- How can communication and information systems be improved?
- How can we integrate the results of the audit into the budgeting cycle?

furthest along this path as it has embarked on a stakeholder-focused, quantitative, and comprehensive social audit. At the same time, it is grappling with how it will incorporate the audit results into its existing strategic management and budgeting systems. The VanCity Credit Union experience offers insight into where the field of social accounting is going.

VanCity Credit Union's foray into social accounting began in 1992 when its board of directors decided to broaden the scope of the corporation's annual report to include more information about the credit union's social performance. This decision was based on the fact that the credit union was ranked below many of the larger banks for its level of disclosure in a study by the Society of Management Accountants of Canada. The credit union had a long history of strong community reinvestment and support and had expected to excel in this area. Also, as a member-owned, locally based financial organization, it felt it had an obligation to report on socially responsible community initiatives.

The next two years saw VanCity Credit Union move toward more complete reporting of its progress in meeting its social goals and objectives. Its 1996 annual report, for example, covered its activities relating to community economic development lending, volunteerism, job creation, environmental impact, employee benefits and compensation, training, and equity.

Beginning in 1997, VanCity Credit Union undertook a more comprehensive social audit with the help of the New Economics Foundation of Great Britain. Using its management philosophy and mission statement as the starting point for the assessment, the VanCity social audit team identified key stakeholders, met with groups of managers to develop indicators of social performance, benchmarked "best practices" in and outside the industry, and held focus groups with employees, customers, and other credit union leaders to assess their views on their relationships with VanCity Credit Union and to identify important social responsibility issues and values. It also looked at its management systems to identify barriers and problems from the point of view of improving its overall social performance.

During the focus groups, the audit process was explained and feedback was gathered on how the credit union's performance was perceived. Participants were also asked to identify important social performance issues that they thought the credit union should focus on.

Another important feature of the audit was the review of the credit union's management systems and structures. Meetings were held with small groups of managers to identify systemic and structural barriers to improved social performance. This critical stage of the audit examines organizational systems such as those that regulate information sharing, communication, decision making, performance assessment, rewards and recognition, and accountability.

Later in 1998, when the first full social audit report is expected to be released, VanCity Credit Union will begin to examine how it will integrate the audit process into its strategic management system, from using the results in budgeting to incorporating corporate social performance objectives into employee evaluations. It intends to continue the dialogue with stakeholders and use that process to more fully engage members, employees, suppliers, and other stakeholders in improving its overall social performance.

Define the Purpose and Scope of the Stakeholder Audit

BUILD SENIOR MANAGEMENT COMMITMENT

Interest in conducting a stakeholder audit often arises naturally out of the relationship-building process. Finding ways to assess the effectiveness of the relationship-building initiatives and to solicit and respond to stakeholder feedback are important elements of an overall strategic program to build stakeholder relationships.

If a company has not taken on relationship building as a strategic direction, an internal "champion" such as the CEO or member of the board of directors may inspire interest in measuring corporate social performance.

The stakeholder-audit champion may develop an initial plan for raising organizational awareness and then set up a meeting to discuss the issue and win commitment to proceed with the audit. This meeting, sometimes using a workshop format with outside experts, introduces senior management to the purpose and definition of social accounting and outlines the experiences of others, the steps involved in conducting a stakeholder audit, and the range of approaches and methodologies. Useful questions to ask at this stage include the following:

- Why is our organization interested in monitoring social performance?
- How can the stakeholder audit be integrated within our overall relationship-building initiative?
- Who is the social accounting and auditing process for?
- What kind of an audit report does our organization need?
- How broadly will it be communicated?

FORM AUDIT COMMITTEE

The next step is to form a cross-functional task force to lead the design and implementation of the audit. The task force should include business units and staff from core functions such as marketing, human resources, planning, and communications. Involving representatives from all levels and areas of the company will avoid creating resentment about the extra work involved in data collecting and overcome resistance and skepticism that may develop as a result.

One of the most important roles of task force members is to share information about the company's social performance goals and the audit process with others in their division. Building enthusiasm for improving the company's social performance is critical. If people see the relevance and value of social auditing, they will be much more willing to contribute to the audit tasks.

The task force should also decide whether to hire an independent researcher to assist with the design and implementation of the audit. Because the skills required to design and conduct a stakeholder audit are varied and specialized (i.e., designing questionnaires and moderating focus groups), having outside help can be a boon. Also, an independent researcher can ensure that feedback from employees and other stakeholders is as free from bias as possible.

DEVELOP AUDIT IMPLEMENTATION PLAN

The first major job of the audit task force is to develop an implementation plan. The plan will lay out exactly how the stakeholder audit process will be undertaken and should specify the audit objectives, process, schedule, budget, roles and responsibilities, and reporting arrangements. It should also specify when the audit year will end. Ideally, the audit cycle should end at the same time as the financial year. This will help integrate the financial and stakeholder audit results.

SELECTING STAKEHOLDER GROUPS TO BE INVOLVED IN THE AUDIT

Deciding on the level of stakeholder participation and selecting the groups to be involved is a crucial step in audit design. One major purpose of an audit is to understand and take account of the perspectives of each of the organization's major stakeholder groups, to identify issues of importance to them, and to listen effectively. There are two distinct roles for stakeholder participants: the first is to contribute to the formulation of stakeholder strategies, and the second is to provide feedback on the results contained in the audit report—answering surveys, participating in focus groups, and so on.

Choosing which stakeholder groups should be involved in the audit needs to be done carefully and in the context of the company's broader relationship-building strategy. It requires that a company look at how its activities affect internal and external groups as well as which external groups currently affect its activities. In prioritizing stakeholder groups, the task force could choose groups that are central to the mission and values of the organization or those with whom the organization most directly and frequently interacts. An organization can also consider the stakeholder's power, legitimacy, and the urgency of its claims. See chapter 4 for a fuller discussion of the issues of selecting priority stakeholders.

Some companies begin by including only employees in the first round of the audit and add other groups in later years. To save time and resources during the first or second audit cycle, it is usually beneficial to limit the number of stakeholders involved to between two and five. This will minimize the complexity of the audit process. Keep in mind that gathering stakeholder views every year is time consuming and costly.

Ideally, after several audit cycles, all major stakeholders should be involved, including those whose feedback may be critical. Being open to feedback from stakeholders who are critical is difficult, but they may provide the most useful input and lead to the greatest benefit for the company. Because the actions of a company can simultaneously benefit one stakeholder group while harming another, there will always be some stakeholders who have a more positive perspective than others.

Exhibit 5: A List of Potential Stakeholders

- employees
- retired employees
- customers
- stockholders and investors
- suppliers
- residents of local communities
- industry associations
- competitors
- government regulators
- the general public

Clarify Social Mission, Values, and Goals

A stakeholder audit should be designed with reference to an organization's strategy, values, and goals. Some companies may have already articulated their social mission and goals. In most companies, however, stakeholder goals have not been identified explicitly, and if they do exist, they are not well integrated with financial goals. Employees haven't been involved in developing the corporate vision and strategies, and they don't have a clear idea of what these goals mean for their own behavior, knowledge that is critical in establishing meaningful individual and team performance targets.

If the goals and strategies are not widely understood and supported throughout the organization, the capacity to harness the creative and productive energy of employees and other key stakeholders in the drive to improve social performance is sharply reduced. This is a key stage of the process that is often skipped over, causing difficulties later on.

When this stage of clarifying corporate values and stakeholder goals is ignored, a stakeholder audit will be more time consuming and improvements in corporate social performance less dramatic. Considerable time will be spent defining and revising performance measures as managers strive to clarify goals and strategies. See chapter 5 for more details.

Perform Baseline Assessment and Gap Analysis

The third step involves gaining a clearer baseline picture of (1) your company's existing stakeholder relationships, (2) "best practices" in the industry, (3) corporate strengths and weaknesses (ideally based on dialogue with stakeholders), and (4) gaps and liabilities. Typically, a baseline assessment covers topics such as corporate community involvement, employee relations, diversity, environment, international relationships, and marketplace practices.

A major purpose of this stage is to identify potential "hot spots" in social performance that may require immediate attention. The assessment should begin with a review of management practices and existing policies and programs to identify gaps and liabilities.

REVIEWING INTERNAL POLICIES AND PRACTICES

Guidelines for Corporate Social Performance, a manual developed by Canadian Business for Social Responsibility, provides an easy-to-use format for conducting a baseline audit. The guidelines are essentially a checklist that companies can use as a starting point for assessing gaps, liabilities, and strengths.[1] Because each company has its own goals that are influenced by stakeholder expectations, each company's criteria will also be unique.

BENCHMARKING BEST PRACTICES

Benchmarks are points of reference or comparisons that are used to stimulate innovation and improvement. Benchmarking can help to identify "best practices." For example, another company may have developed strong relationships with its community stakeholders. Finding out more about how that company built the relationship and the activities that have contributed most to that relationship could help to stimulate changes in your own operation. Benchmarking is covered in more detail in chapter 7.

The next step is to develop strategies for improving corporate social performance by establishing and maintaining positive, collaborative relationships with key stakeholders. This step is included here as a reminder that a major purpose of the audit is to help organizations improve their social relationships.

Figure 7
*List of Sample Indicators: Canadian Business for Social
Responsibility's* Guidelines for Corporate Social Performance, *1997*

Community development
- A statement of the company's commitment to the community is publicly available.
- Information is provided to staff and suppliers on social and community issues.
- Work placements and internships are offered in partnership with local educational institutions.
- One percent of pretax profits is donated to charitable organizations.
- Priority is given to local employees and suppliers.
- Twenty percent of the annual donation budget is allocated to local CED projects, such as job-skills training, job-creation programs, and programs to encourage self-sufficiency.

Diversity
- Compliance with the Charter of Rights or U.S. equivalent is ensured.
- Pay equity and employment equity (fairness in hiring and promotion) are ensured.
- Equal access to bidding is guaranteed for all suppliers.
- Compliance with the Employee Standards Act is ensured.
- Performance reviews for employees and contract employees are two-way.
- Payment and bonus policies are freely communicated.
- A profit-sharing/bonus package is available.
- Suppliers receive prompt payment.

Clear two-way communication
- A suggestion program is available and used.
- Explicit, nondiscriminatory guidelines for promotion are freely communicated.
- Professional development is supported.
- Explicit information is provided on benefits.
- The termination policy is fair and explicit.
- Alternatives to downsizing are explored.
- Flexible work hours are permitted.

Environment
- Compliance with environmental laws and regulations is ensured.
- An environmental policy statement is available.
- Policies to reduce environmental impacts are in place, with training.
- Communication occurs inside and outside the corporation about environmental initiatives.
- Preference is given to environmentally responsible suppliers.
- One or more employees are responsible for environmental programs.
- Other employees are also involved.

continues on next page

Figure 7 (cont.)
List of Sample Indicators: Canadian Business for Social Responsibility's Guidelines for Corporate Social Performance, *1997*

International relationships
- Compliance with human rights legislation is ensured.
- Employee and environmental standards are applied in international operations.
- Preference is given to local suppliers.
- No child or prison labor is used to produce goods or services.
- Local communities are not displaced.

Marketplace practices
- Compliance with consumer protection laws and regulations is ensured.
- Advertising is truthful.
- Customer satisfaction policies are explicitly stated.
- Payment of suppliers is fair and timely.
- A code of ethics is in place.
- A dispute resolution process is available and used.

Fiscal responsibility
- Financial resources are managed to ensure long-term fiscal viability.
- Audits are conducted to ensure accountability.
- Social and environmental policies are reviewed regularly.
- Progress toward stated goals is measured and reported.
- Concerns of employees and the public are anticipated and responded to regarding social and environmental hazards and impacts.

Case Study: Using Baseline Audit Results to Improve Performance
While it sounds simple to apply the results of a baseline audit, it is often not the case. For example, a baseline audit conducted for a bank we will call People's Bank, confirmed that the bank had developed a purchasing policy that gave preference to environmentally responsible suppliers. While this fact was positively scored on the baseline audit, it did not translate into improved performance (e.g., sustainable environmental practices and enhanced reputation) because purchasing staff members were not aware of the criteria used by the company to define an environmentally responsible supplier, did not have a list of such suppliers, or did not understand how they were expected to make trade-offs against cost in the procurement process. Most importantly, they were not rewarded for finding environmentally responsible suppliers and therefore their motivation

to comply remained low. As a result of the baseline audit, the company had the information it needed to improve its performance in the socially responsible purchasing arena.

Develop Social-Performance Measures

The next task is to decide how to measure your organization's progress in meeting its stakeholder goals and objectives. Companies that have already developed clear goals and strategies will find it much easier to decide on appropriate indicators and annual targets.

Case Study: From Social Goals to Targets

A fictitious oil and gas company decided it wanted to improve its relationships with several communities where it operated by becoming a "neighbor of choice." Its strategies for achieving this social goal included dealing with community concerns about environmental impacts by installing new emission control devices, improving communication with local citizens by holding several dialogue sessions, and increasing local benefits by hiring more local residents.

With respect to the environmental strategy, carbon dioxide (CO_2) emissions were selected as an indicator with a target of 15 percent reduction over twelve months. The indicator for improved communication was increased public support as measured through a public opinion survey of residents, with a target of an increased approval rating of one point. The indicator for increasing local benefits was the number of local residents hired, and the target was five new hires per year.

It is important that managers responsible for implementing corporate strategies are involved in selecting indicators and targets. This will increase the appropriateness of the measures and also managers' commitment to collecting data and improving their own and the company's performance. Involving stakeholders in a review of indicators and targets has also been found to be helpful in generating better measures and more support for the results of the audit.

Indicators, or measures of performance, are identified for each stakeholder goal. Consider one of Ben and Jerry's goals, "to be clear with franchisees about their role ... and to provide them with consistent, useful technical and logistical support." A measure or indicator for that goal might be the awareness levels of franchisees, or their satisfaction with the information and logistical support received from the head office. Establishing targets for performance allows a company to identify and move toward its desired level of performance. Targets should change from year to year as progress is made.

Generally, a mix of qualitative and quantitative indicators is recommended. For example, actual dollar figures for salaries as well as the perceptions of staff about the fairness of rates, rates of increase or decrease over five years, and comparisons with other similar companies will give more information than any one measure alone. Ideally, indicators should be easy to understand and meaningful to both the company and its stakeholders. Stakeholders' expectations are important. Involve them in selecting criteria and indicators so that the results will be meaningful and credible.

Design a Social Performance Monitoring System

Once indicators and targets have been identified, existing sources of data should be reviewed and gaps identified. In many cases, companies already collect some of the information needed for a stakeholder audit.

At this stage, the oil and gas company asked questions such as "Do we already track CO_2 emissions? Do we conduct an annual community survey, and if so, are there appropriate questions related to reputation? Do we know where new employees lived and worked prior to joining the firm?"

Once you know what data or information you already collect, you can design a more comprehensive monitoring system. Decide what else needs to be measured, what the appropriate indicators are, who will collect the data, and what form it will be in. Experts in the field suggest that the best results come from using multiple sources of information to measure the impact of corporate activities on their stakeholders.

The internal audit task force should take the lead in exploring and then selecting appropriate research methods. Deciding on an appropriate mix of research methods will depend on resources and time available, the scope of the audit, and the preferences of stakeholders.

For example, using a self-completed survey to obtain feedback from employees may not result in a very high return rate. Holding a series of focus groups led by an independent moderator may generate broadly based input, but it will cost more. Depending on the type of research expertise within your organization, you may wish to seek external advice.

Consulting with stakeholders prior to deciding on the research methodology will also help to avoid difficulties later on. Customers, for example, will prefer a method that minimizes the time they are required to spend. They will have fewer concerns than employees about confidentiality.

Stakeholders should also be consulted about the questions to be covered in the research and the measures being used—for instance, contributions to the community or employee benefits. This is important for building credibility for the audit and the company. If stakeholders believe that the questions asked were too narrow or were biased, they will have very little confidence in the audit results. Asking for their input early in the process will increase their commitment to the audit as well as their willingness to participate.

At this stage, the company must commit to conducting more than one round of dialogue—that is, to commit to sharing the results of the audit with the stakeholders who are consulted and obtaining their feedback on the results.

SELECT RESEARCH TECHNIQUES

The following research tools are most often used in stakeholder audits.

POLICY AND DOCUMENT ANALYSIS

A major source of information for stakeholder audits comes from the company's own records, including its corporate mission and social values statement, documents such as minutes of board meetings, policy statements, interdepartmental correspondence, records, files, and memoranda. Employee performance review forms, the organization's business plan, and its annual report are also prime sources of content, including financial data.

Records, reports, and other publications prepared by outside organizations about the company's performance are another source of valuable information. Media articles, industry rating profiles, and so on, should be considered as input to the audit.

FOCUS GROUPS

Focus groups are one of the most commonly used audit research techniques. Focus groups usually involve eight to ten individuals in a discussion lasting between ninety minutes and two hours. A moderator, ideally not an employee of the company, facilitates the discussion and poses open-ended questions about how company policies or initiatives affect members of the group. The moderator also guides the discussion and helps the group maintain its focus. Focus groups are often used to identify the issues that should be addressed in surveys. Selecting a representative group of individuals from the larger stakeholder group is essential.

While senior managers often watch focus groups from behind a one-way mirror when they are being conducted for market research purposes, this may not be advisable for an audit—respondents may be less likely to be open with their comments if they know a company manager is observing.

INTERVIEWS

Interviews with stakeholders are also a staple of the research techniques used for audits. Interviews ideally contain a mix of structured and open-ended questions. Particularly during the first one or two audit cycles, efforts should be made to identify issues that are important to the stakeholders. An interviewer (ideally an independent researcher or auditor) will use probing and triangulation as methods for verifying responses from one person to the next. (The meaning of probing is self-explanatory; triangulation involves using the responses of three interviewees to focus on the answer to a question.)

SURVEYS

Surveys are useful when collecting information from more than fifty people. For example, questionnaires are often used to gather input from suppliers who are in remote locations or to survey large numbers of employees or customers. The design of the questionnaire and the development of questions that ensure coverage of all important issues can determine the usefulness of a survey.

MEETINGS AND FACILITATED WORKSHOPS

To gather input from community representatives, some form of "town hall" meeting or workshop is often appropriate. Although it is becoming increasingly difficult to get members of the public to attend forums, their participation can be encouraged if the sponsor directly affects their lives and the community and if they perceive that the sponsoring company is honestly looking for feedback to improve its relationships with the community.

Calling representatives of key community organizations ahead of time to encourage them to attend, setting concrete goals for the meeting, inviting a guest speaker, or tying the meeting in with an existing community function can all increase attendance and ensure a representative gathering.

Instead of community meetings, an ad hoc committee can be established with representatives from the range of stakeholder categories. In selecting representatives for this more focused dialogue, ensure that information is available about the company's activities that are of concern. Representatives should also have credibility within the broader community. Usually an advisory committee of between six and ten people is ideal.

SET UP A SOCIAL BOOKKEEPING SYSTEM

Collecting and organizing information for the stakeholder audit should be planned on an annual basis. The first step is to set up a "social bookkeeping" system. Good social bookkeepers will collect and include both qualitative and quantitative information; they will ensure that data is accurate, complete, straightforward, and efficient to collect and analyze. Also important is ensuring that the individuals who gather the data understand its relevance to the audit and the goal of improving stakeholder relationships.

In most cases, starting small in the audit's first year will pay off. Select a few indicators for which data can be collected easily and then add to the list in year two. Remember the phrase, "garbage in, garbage out." Select only meaningful measures and reduce the number of indicators to the most relevant.

The following specific tasks must be undertaken in the data-collection process:

• Decide what information needs to be collected and how often.

- Identify sources.

- Decide who will record and collect the information.

- Decide how records will be kept and their format. (Will a computer be used or a record book completed manually?)

- Monitor recordkeeping and ensure that records are being kept and that problems are resolved.

- Establish links between records and management decision-making processes.

- Communicate summaries of information to staff to keep up their enthusiasm and to show relevance to the company's mission.

Prepare a Stakeholder Audit Report

Usually the social bookkeeping system needs to be established and data collected for approximately one year before a stakeholder audit report is prepared. Some companies produce an interim report for internal purposes at six months to help avoid surprises at the end of the year and to ensure that all relevant information is being collected.

DATA ANALYSIS AND INTERPRETATION

Once qualitative information has been collected from stakeholders (through focus groups, surveys, and other methods), and quantitative data is compiled and analyzed, it's time to write the stakeholder audit report. Research specialists are available to analyze the data if that expertise is not available internally. The format and content of the report will vary depending on the objectives of the company.

COMMUNICATE RESULTS AND DISCUSS INTERNALLY

Feedback from the stakeholder audit should first go to the functional areas of the organization covered by the audit. The people who manage the relationships with stakeholders should get the first look at the information. This will help reduce any dissonance between their expectations for success and the results and also ensure that staff involved in gathering information and those who can best use the data to improve performance get the information first. Next, a draft of the audit should be presented to senior executives and members of the board of directors.

A detailed audit report should include the company's stakeholder goals and objectives; a description of the audit methodology, measures, and targets; summaries of comments of stakeholders; and recommendations for change.

Review Results with Stakeholders

After the board has reviewed the results, the stakeholder audit report should be shared with external stakeholders, beginning with those who participated in the research. Informal presentations to small groups can be followed by discussions, or an organization can opt for more formal reviews with written feedback. Face-to-face communication and dialogue about the results will go a long way toward helping to build trust and credibility.

Finally, broader distribution of the audit report can be achieved by incorporating it into the annual report. Some companies, such as The Body Shop, publish separate summary reports since the full stakeholder audit tends to be very long.

While some companies find disclosure of the results difficult, often this is the most valuable part of the process. Feedback from stakeholders can be used to revise corporate goals and strategies, and refine objectives and measures.

Align Corporate Systems and Structures

USE THE RESULTS TO IMPROVE SOCIAL PERFORMANCE AND PLAN FOR THE NEXT AUDIT CYCLE

The results of the audit should be integrated in the corporate strategic planning process to ensure there is ongoing or continuous improvement in stakeholder relationships. In addition, a debriefing session with researchers and staff can be useful to identify ways to improve the audit process itself.

The stakeholder audit process and results should provide a mechanism to identify structural and system barriers and problem areas, design appropriate individual and divisional performance targets, and develop meaningful reward and recognition systems. Without appropriate structures and rewards systems to support employees, their efforts will likely not be sustained, and performance against crucial corporate goals will suffer.

Stakeholder Auditing and Performance Management

In conclusion, to be most effective, a stakeholder audit should be designed and conducted as part of a strategic management system. This more integrated approach will increase the effectiveness and impact of the stakeholder audit by

- ensuring that corporate social performance measures are accurate and appropriate
- increasing understanding and support of the stakeholder goals and objectives among employees and other stakeholders
- ensuring that intangible drivers of social performance are considered in strategic planning and budgeting decisions
- creating rewards and recognition structures that are linked to meeting individual and team stakeholder objectives and targets
- providing an ongoing cycle of dialogue and reporting that will ultimately build both credibility and trust

The Future of Corporate-
Stakeholder Relations

Establishing a good reputation, trusting relationships with suppliers, strong community linkages, and responsible environmental practices will help ensure the long-term profitability and sustainability of your company. While business leaders are beginning to look beyond financial performance at these more intangible drivers of long-term success, this movement has only just begun.

Management attention is shifting from internal business practices to an awareness of the importance of a business's external environment. Total Quality Management, with its focus on customer satisfaction, was the first stage. The recently popularized concept of the learning organization heralds a further extension of management's concern away from the concrete elements of workplace design into the relatively "soft" area of employee learning and growth.

I believe that the next wave will be the network of long-term relationships a company establishes with its external and internal stakeholders, the values that support those relationships, and the processes that are needed to build and maintain them.

Firms with a compelling sense of direction, a strong set of values and beliefs, and a web of collaborative stakeholder relationships will thrive in our increasingly turbulent, competitive, global economy. Intense cooperation rather than competition will be the ticket to survival.

Companies that demonstrate pro-social values and create dynamic, high-involvement workplaces will be able to attract and retain highly skilled knowledge workers. Relationships with customers, suppliers, and the public will provide companies with a vital source of information and contribute to higher levels of trust, lower costs, and a greater capacity for innovation. Finally, positive stakeholder relationships will create a reservoir of goodwill and a solid reputation, both critical to maintaining customer loyalty and shareholder value. Management attention will be on stakeholder relationships because they *are* the next source of competitive advantage.

It's a New World

This new world is not just around the corner, leaving us a decade or so to change and adapt. In many ways the future is already here. The idea that the impact of change is overestimated in the short term and underestimated in the longer term is particularly relevant at this stage in history. Experts predicted that new technology, particularly advances in computers and telecommunications, would have a drastic impact on business. These changes have not materialized, in the short term, to the extent that everyone expected.

However, the more profound impacts of technological change and the ensuing changes in social attitudes and behavior are about to be unleashed upon the business community. Democratized, instant communication means that corporations can no longer control their reputations—everything about a company including what goes on inside the company's walls can and will be communicated. Knowledge workers, in demand and mobile, will choose to work for companies whose values are aligned with their own. Compatible relationships with co-workers will be the deciding factor for employees that command a good salary wherever they go. The public that has supported the devolution of government and its powers to regulate, will scrutinize corporate behavior as never before. As shareholders and media-savvy citizens they will wield considerable power.

Companies are already being pressured to offer paid employee volunteer time, a reduced work week, a reduction in pay differentials between CEOs and top-level employees, and to include employees and other stakeholders on boards of directors. These demands for corporate stakeholder responsibility will continue to escalate in the coming decade.

What's a Company to Do?

This book presents a model that companies can use to build a network of positive, collaborative stakeholder relationships that will be essential for success in this new economy. The longevity and effectiveness of these relationships will depend on five areas of corporate competence: the ability to listen well, to monitor and measure intangible aspects of performance, to align corporate values with stakeholder values, to balance diverse interests, and to continuously improve relationships by incorporating feedback into corporate strategic management systems.

Companies that develop their capability to listen effectively will tap into vital pools of information that will allow them to respond quickly and deftly. Listening will not be relegated to one or two employees or to passive information-gathering systems. All employees will be part of a team and will need to develop the skills and motivation to seek information and clarification from their colleagues and other partners. They will also need to listen for what is really being said, to interpret cross-cultural differences in meaning, and to deal with that information in a nonreactive and nonjudgmental way. Organizations will need to develop multiway, face-to-face and electronic communication systems to ensure that this knowledge is available and used.

New nonasset-based measures of performance will be needed to enable companies to manage intangibles like reputation, employee satisfaction, and consumer loyalty. Boards of directors, shareholders, and interested citizens will demand that companies monitor and measure the impact of the firm's actions on all stakeholders, not just shareholders. This pressure for greater accountability will lead businesses toward more rigorous and comprehensive social accounting and reporting. Companies that are able to accurately measure performance using a broad mix of financial as well as nonfinancial indicators and communicate that information in a transparent and open fashion will be able to manage better. They will also enhance their reputation and their stakeholder relationships.

Companies that align their values with those of their stakeholders will be able to withstand the vagaries of consumer behavior and the slings and arrows of mass-media attention. Shared values between a company and its employees, customers, suppliers, and communities will serve as a foundation upon which trusting, long-term relationships can be built. These shared values will also be a source of corporate strength and resilience.

The ability to balance the interests of all stakeholders will be a defining characteristic of successful companies in the next decade. This is not to say that companies will be able to satisfy everyone's interests all the time. However, companies that have a strong set of values and that can communicate their business goals clearly will maintain stakeholders' support even when the results are not in their favor. This is because most people judge the fairness of a decision not only according to how the "pie" is divided but also, and more importantly, according to whether the decision was arrived at through a fair and equitable process.

Finally, companies will need to develop a more balanced approach to monitoring and managing their overall performance. Stronger connections will need to be made between social accounting and strategic planning and budgeting to ensure that a company's actions support its social as well as financial goals. Using an integrated approach to stakeholder auditing, companies will be able to monitor and continuously improve their stakeholder relationships and thereby assure competitiveness in the short as well as long term.

Notes

CHAPTER 1: WHY BUILD COLLABORATIVE STAKEHOLDER
RELATIONSHIPS?

1. Steven Prokesch, "Unleashing the Power of Learning: An Interview with British Petroleum's John Browne," *Harvard Business Review* (September/October 1997): 154.

2. Reginald A. Litz, (1996) "A Resource Based View of the Socially Responsible Firm: Stakeholder Interdependence, Ethical Awareness and Issue Responsiveness as Strategic Assets," *Journal of Business Ethics* 15 (1966): 1355-1363.

3. Timothy Egan, "Microsoft Swagger Taking a Hit," *Vancouver Sun* (January 17, 1998): page C-1.

4. John Entine, "Shattered Image: Is The Body Shop Too Good to Be True?" *Business Ethics* (September/October 1994): 23-28.

5. "The Road Ahead: A Summary of The Body Shop Values Report," (Littlehampton, England: The Body Shop International, 1997): 1.

6. Worldwatch Institute, *Vital Signs* (New York: W.W. Norton, 1996).

7. R. Bennett, *International Business* (London: Pitman Publishing, 1996).

8. Neil Nevitte and Mebs Kanji, "From Materialism to Postmaterialism: A New Set of Values for a New Century," *Canadian Journal of Marketing Research* 16 (1997): 12-20.

9. W. Orts, "Beyond Shareholders: Interpreting Corporate Constituency Statutes," *The George Washington Law Review* 61, no. 1 (1992): 14-135.

10. Peter Pruzan, "The Ethical Dimensions of Banking: Sbn Bank, Denmark," in Simon Zadek, Peter Pruzan, and Richard Evans, eds., *Building Corporate Accountability: Emerging Practices in Social and Ethical Accounting, Auditing and Reporting* (London: Earthscan Publications Ltd., 1997).

11. J. Charkham, *Keeping Good Company: A Study of Corporate Governance in Five Countries* (Oxford: Oxford University Press, 1995).

12. Donna Wood, "Corporate Social Performance Revisited," *Academy of Management Review* (October 1991): 691-717.

CHAPTER 2: STAKEHOLDER COLLABORATION AND THE BOTTOM LINE

1. See Curtis Verschoor, "Principles Build Profits," *Management Accounting* (October 1997): 42; J. Griffin and J. Mahon, "The Corporate Social Performance and Corporate Financial Performance Debate," *Business and Society* (March 1997): 5-31; and J. C. Collins and J. I. Porras, *Built to Last:*

Successful Habits of Visionary Companies (London: Century, Random House, 1995).

2. Donna Wood, "Stakeholder Mismatching: A Theoretical Problem in Empirical Research on Corporate Social Performance," *The International Journal of Organizational Analysis* 3, no. 3 (1995): 229-267.

3. Sandra Waddock and Samuel Graves, "Quality of Management in Quality of Stakeholder Relations," *Business and Society* 36, 3 (September 1997).

4. John Kotter and James Heskett, *Corporate Culture and Performance* (New York: Free Press, 1992).

5. Max Clarkson, "Good Business and the Bottom Line," *Canadian Business Magazine* (May 1991): 28.

6. Larue Tone Hosmer, "Response to 'Do Good Ethics Always Make for Good Business?'" *Strategic Management Journal* 17 (1996): 501.

7. Margaret Blair, *Ownership and Control: Rethinking Corporate Governance for the Twentieth Century* (1995), in M. Clarkson, ed., *The Corporation and Its Stakeholders: Classic and Contemporary Readings* (Washington, D.C.: Brookings Institution, 1997).

8. John Dalla Costa, *Working Wisdom: The Ultimate Value in the New Economy* (Toronto: Stoddard Publishing, 1995).

9. Robert Walker, "The Ethical Imperative," *The Financial Post 500 Magazine* (1997): 28.

10. "Does It Pay to Be Ethical?" *Business Ethics Magazine* (March/April 1997): 14.

11. Cone/Roper. *Cause Related Marketing Trends Report* (1997).

12. The Market Vision Group, Market Vision 2000 Consumer Attitudes towards Corporations Operating in Canada, 1995.

13. Don Peppers and Martha Rogers, "Lessons from the Front: Five Companies That Have What It Takes to Become a 1:1 Enterprise," *Marketing Tools* (January/February 1998): 39.

14. Ibid.

15. Cited in Paul N. Bloom, Pattie Yu Hussein, and Lisa R. Szykman, "Benefiting Society and the Bottom Line: Businesses Emerge from the Shadows to Promote Social Causes," *Marketing Management* 4, no. 3 (winter 1995): 8.

16. Cited by Carol Cone, Cone Communications, in "Execs View Cause Marketing As a Way to Build Relationships," *Marketing News* (August 26, 1996): 8.

17. The full text of the study can be found on the Social Investment Forum's website at www.socialinvest.org.

18. *San Francisco Chronicle* (November 6, 1997): D3.

19. Leslie Wines, "High Order Strategy for Manufacturing," *Journal of Business Strategy* (July/August 1996): 32.

20. James Champy and Nitin Nohria, eds. *Fast Forward: The Best Ideas on Managing Business Change* (Boston: Harvard Business School Press, 1996).

21. Thomas M. Jones, "Instrumental Stakeholder Theory: A Synthesis of Ethics and Economics," *Academy of Management Review* 20, no. 2 (1995): 404-437.

22. John H. Sheridan, "Bonds of Trust," *Industry Week,* March 1997, p. 52.

23. Richard Normann and Rafael Ramirez, "From Value Chain to Value Constellation: Designing Interactive Strategy," *Harvard Business Review* (July/August 1993): 65-77

24. *Business Week* (May 26, 1997): 88.

25. Richard Barrett, "Liberating the Corporate Soul," *HR Focus* (April 1997): 15.

26. http://www.seafirstbank.com/sf_community.html.

27. *Financial Times* (August 10, 1997): 22.

28. *Utne Reader* (July/August 1997): 14

29. *Ethikos* (September/October 1997): 8.

30. *HR Magazine* (June 1997): 110.

31. *Fortune* (June 9, 1997): 168.

32. Stuart Hart, "Beyond Greening: Strategies for a Sustainable World," *Harvard Business Review* (January/February 1997): 66.

33. "How Dupont Is Turning Sustainability into an Engine of Profitability," *Green Business Letter* (October 1997).

34. Ajay Menon and Anil Menon, "Enviropreneurial Marketing Strategy: The Emergence of Corporate Environmentalism as Market Strategy," *Journal of Marketing* 61 (January 1997): 54.

35. Ray Anderson, in an "Off the Record" interview, April 11, 1996. The interview can be found at http://www.nitco.com/users/schumm/schumm.html.

36. Willis Harman, *Why Is There a World Business Academy?* (Washington, D.C.: World Business Academy Ltd., 1991).

37. Richard Barrett, *Liberating the Corporate Soul: Building a Visionary Organization* (Woburn, Mass.: Butterworth-Heinemann, 1998).

CHAPTER 3: A MODEL FOR CORPORATE-STAKEHOLDER RELATIONS

1. M. Jensen and W. Meckling. "Theory of the Firm: Managerial Behaviour, Agency Costs, and Ownership Structure," *Journal of Financial Economics* 3 (1976): 305-60.

2. Anthony Atkinson, John Waterhouse, and Robert A. Wells, "Stakeholder Approach to Strategic Performance Measurement," *Sloan Management Review* (spring 1997): 25.

3. L.G. Telser, "A Theory of Self-Enforcing Agreements," *Journal of Business* 53 (1980): 27-44.

4. I. Macneil, *The New Social Contract: An Inquiry into Modern Contractual Relations.* (New Haven: Yale University Press, 1980).

5. Claudia Gonella and Robert Beckett "Visualising and Measuring Intellectual Performance—The Skandia Approach," *Accountability Quarterly* 6 (1998): 7.

6. See Max Clarkson, ed., *The Corporation and its Stakeholders: Classic and Contemporary Readings* (Toronto: University of Toronto Press, 1998).

7. Ronald K. Mitchell, Bradley R. Agle, and Donna J. Wood, "Toward a Theory of Stakeholder Identification and Salience: Defining the Principle of Who and What Really Counts," *Academy of Management Review* 22, no. 4 (1997): 853-886.

8. Thomas Donaldson and Lee Preston, "Redefining the Corporation," in Max Clarkson, ed., *The Corporation and Its Stakeholders: Classic and Contemporary Readings* (Toronto: University of Toronto Press, 1998): vii.

9. James Moore, *The Death of Competition* (New York: Harper Collins Publishers, Inc., 1996).

10. James Kennelly, "Quantum Leaps and Small Surprises: Stakeholder Theory and the New Science," *1995 Proceedings of the Business in Society Conference* (manuscript provided by author, 1995): 91-96.

11. Dr. Robert Boutilier, my business partner, and I have worked with VanCity Credit Union as external consultants over the past eight years to design and implement this program. We worked most directly with the vice president of marketing and planning, the manager of advertising and promotion, and more recently with the manager of corporate social responsibility. Over the years, we also made a number of presentations to the board of directors and helped to facilitate the involvement of staff relationship-building committees.

12. A delphi process is an iterative research method. A group of "experts" is surveyed and the results of the survey are tabulated and given back to the respondents, who then revise their own responses based on this feedback from the larger group.

CHAPTER 4: A GUIDE TO FOSTERING STAKEHOLDER RELATIONSHIPS

1. William Isaacs, "Taking Flight: Dialogue, Collective Thinking and Organizational Learning," *Organizational Dynamics* 22 no. 2, 1993): 24-39.

2. David B. Guralink, ed., *Websters New World Dictionary: Second College Edition* (New York: Prentice Hall Press, 1986) 550.

3. Jeanne Liedtka, "Collaborating across Lines of Business for Competitive Advantage," *Academy of Management Executive Journal* 10, no. 2 (1996): 20-37.

4. Barbara Gray, *Collaborating: Finding Common Ground for Multiparty Problems* (San Francisco: Jossey Bass, 1989).

5. Patricia Graham, *Mary P. Follett: The Prophet of Management* (Boston: Harvard Business School Press, 1996).

CHAPTER 5: CORPORATE MISSION, VALUES, AND ETHICS—A FOUNDATION FOR RELATIONSHIP BUILDING

1. As published on Nortel's website: www.nortel.com/cool/environ/EHS_Report.
2. Fred Kofman and Peter Senge. "Communities of Commitment: The Heart of Learning Organizations," *Organizational Dynamics* 22, no. 2 (1993): 5-23.
3. "Does it Pay to be Ethical?" *Business Ethics Magazine* (March/April 1997): 14.
4. Lynn Sharp Paine, "Managing for Organizational Integrity," *Harvard Business Review* (March/April 1994): 106-117
5. Joseph L. Badaracco, Jr., and Allen Webb, "Business Ethics: A View From the Trenches," *California Management Review* (January 1995): 8.
6. Richard LeBlanc, "Codes of Conduct: A State of the Art," presentation at the Canadian Center for Ethics and Corporate Policy, Toronto (October 1996).
7. Elizabeth Pinchot, "Can We Afford Ethics?" *Executive Excellence* (March 1992).
8. Rushworth Kidder, *Shared Values for a Troubled World* (New York: Simon and Schuster, 1994).

CHAPTER 6: ALIGNING CORPORATE SYSTEMS AND STRUCTURES

1. R. Ashkenas, D. Ulrich, T. Jick, and S. Kerr, *The Boundaryless Organization: Breaking the Chains of Organizational Structure.* (San Francisco: Jossey-Bass Publishers, 1995).
2. J. Davis, D. Schoorman, and L. Donaldson. "Towards a Stewardship Theory of Management," *Academy of Management Review* 22, no. 1 (1997): 20-47.
3. Robert Miles, *Managing the Corporate Social Environment: A Grounded Theory* (Englewood Cliffs, New Jersey: Prentice-Hall, 1987).
4. Denis Collins, "How and Why Participatory Management Improves a Company's Social Performance," *Business and Society* 35, no. 2 (June 1996): 176-210.
5. Frank Sonnenberg, *Managing with a Conscience* (New York: McGraw Hill Inc., 1994).
6. *HR News* (December 1997): 4.
7. John Henderson, "Plugging into Strategic Partnerships: The Critical IS Connection," *Sloan Management Review* (spring 1990): 7-17.
8. Balasubramanian, "Organizational Learning and Information Systems" (1997), http://eies.njit.edu/~333/orglrn.htm.
9. George Stalk, Philip Evans, and Lawrence Shulman, "Competing on Capabilities: The New Rules of Corporate Strategy," *Harvard Business Review* (March/April 1992): 57.
10. J. S. Brown and P. Duguid, "Organizational Learning and Communities-of-Practise: Towards a Unified View of Working, Learning and Innovation," *Organization Science* 2, no. 1 (1991): 40-57.

11. Trudy and Peter Johnson-Lenz, "Groupware and the Great Turning," in Kazimierz Gozdz, ed., *Community Building: Renewing Spirit and Learning in Business* (San Francisco: New Leaders Press, Sterling and Stone Inc., 1995).

12. C. K. Prahalad and G. Hamel, *Competing for the Future* (Boston: Harvard Business School Press, 1994).

13. Jeanne M. Liedtka, "Collaborating across Lines of Business for Competitive Advantage," *Academy of Management Review* 10, no. 2 (1996): 20.

14. Ibid., 23.

15. To protect the anonymity of this organization, its name has been changed.

16. R. Ashkenas, D. Ulrich, T. Jick, and S. Kerr, *The Boundaryless Organization: Breaking the Chains of Organizational Structure* (San Francisco: Jossey-Bass Publishers, 1995).

17. Myriam Laberge, "Whole System Technologies," a presentation to the Service Quality Group, Vancouver (November 1997).

18. *Perspectives, The Conference Model: Approach for Accelerated Work Redesign*, The Axelrod Group, Wilinetti, Ill.

19. This section draws upon ideas found in the following sources: William N. Isaacs, "Taking Flight: Dialogue, Collective Thinking, and Organizational Learning," *Organizational Dynamics* 22, no. 2 (1993): 25; E. Schein, "On Dialogue, Culture, and Organizational Learning," *Organizational Dynamics* 22, no. 2 (1993): 42; G. Gerard and L. Teurfs. "Dialogue and Organizational Transformation," in Gozdz Kazimierz, ed., *Community Building: Renewing Spirit and Learning* (San Francisco: New Leaders Press, Sterling & Stone Inc., 1995): 144; Fred Kofman and Peter Senge, "Communities of Commitment: The Heart of the Learning Organization," *Organizational Dynamics* 22, no. 2 (1993): 16.

20. Joan Saries, "Maintaining a Collective Vision at Odwalla," *At Work* (May/June 1997): 7.

CHAPTER 7: DEVELOPING A STAKEHOLDER STRATEGY

1. Margaret Blair, *Ownership and Control: Rethinking Corporate Governance for the Twentieth Century* (Washington, D.C., Brookings Institution, 1995). Blair's research shows that even for manufacturing firms, physical plant and equipment make up a declining share of assets, while a growing share consists of intangibles like patent rights, brand reputation, service capability, and the ability to innovate and get the next product to market in time. Comparing the asset value of property, plant and equipment (pp&e) for manufacturing and mining firms in the United States between 1982 and 1991 shows that pp&e accounted for 62.3 percent of the market value of the firms in 1982 compared with 37.9 percent of the market value of these firms in 1991.

2. J. Waterhouse and A. Svendsen, "Strategic Performance Monitoring and Management: Using Non-Financial Measures to Improve Corporate Governance." Canadian Institute for Chartered Accountants (1998).

3. Richard Normann and Rafael Ramirez, "From Value Chain to Value Constellation: Designing Interactive Strategy," *Harvard Business Review* (July/August 1993): 73.

4. A. Brandenburger and B. Nalebuff, *Co-Opetition* (New York: Doubleday, 1996).

5. Todd Saxton, "The Effects of Partner and Relationship Characteristics on Alliance Outcomes," *Academy of Management Journal* 40, no. 2 (1997): 443-461.

6. *Annual Report, 1995,* Ben and Jerry's Homemade Ice Cream.

CHAPTER 8: HARNESSING THE POWER OF LONG-TERM RELATIONSHIPS

1. Jeanne M. Logsdon, "Interests and Interdependence in the Formation of Social Problem-Solving Collaborations," *Journal of Applied Behavioral Science* 27, no. 1 (March 1991): 23-37.

2. *Ma-mook Development Corporation: Working to Advance our Economic Interests* (Port Alberni, British Columbia: Ma-Mook Development Corporation, 1997).

3. J. Friend and A. Hickling, *Planning under Pressure* (Oxford: Pergamon, 1987).

4. A. Himmelman, "Rationales and Contexts for Collaboration," in Chris Huxham, ed., *Creating Collaborative Advantage* (Thousand Oaks, Calif.: Sage Publications Ltd., 1996).

5. Hester Eisenstein and Alice Jardine, eds. *The Future of Difference* (New Brunswick: Rutgers University Press, 1990).

6. Kathleen Kelley Reardon and Robert E. Spekman. "Starting Out Right: Negotiation Lessons for Domestic and Cross Cultural Business Alliances," *Business Horizons* (January 1994): 71.

7. Larraine Segil, *Intelligent Business Alliances* (Toronto: Times Business, Random House, 1996).

8. This issue is raised by Chris Huxham in the article "Collaboration and Collaborative Advantage," in Chris Huxham, ed., *Creating Collaborative Advantage* (Thousand Oaks, Calif.: Sage Publications Ltd., 1996).

9. Frank Sonnenberg, *Managing with a Conscience* (New York: McGraw-Hill, Inc., 1994): 180.

10. Larue Hosmer, "Trust: The Connection Link Between Organizational Theory and Philosophical Ethics." *Academy of Management Review* 20, no. 2 (1995): 393.

11. Nirmalya Kumar, "The Power of Trust in Manufacturer-Retailer Relationships," *Harvard Business Review* (November/December 1996): 92-106.

12. Kumar, op. cit.

13. Jan Walsh, "Stakeholder Consultation in BT: Listening and Responding," *Accountability Quarterly* 3 (spring 1997).

CHAPTER 9: SOCIAL ACCOUNTING—AN ESSENTIAL MANAGEMENT TOOL

1. Simon Zadek, ed., *Building Corporate Accountability: Emerging Practices in Social and Ethical Accounting, Auditing and Reporting* (London: Earthscan Publications Ltd., 1997).

2. Carolyn Brancato, "New Corporate Performance Measures," research report no. 1118-95-RR (New York: The Conference Board, 1996).

CHAPTER 10: STAKEHOLDER AUDIT: A TOOL FOR ASSESSING AND IMPROVING STAKEHOLDER RELATIONSHIPS

1. See the *Guidelines for Corporate Social Performance* developed by Canadian Business for Social Responsibility (1977). A copy of the guidelines can be ordered for US$25.00. by calling 604-323-2714. Business for Social Responsibility (U.S.) has also developed a social responsibility starter kit.

About the Author

ANN SVENDSEN, a sociologist, has worked in the stakeholder relations field for over twenty years. During that time, she has helped a variety of businesses and government agencies forge stronger, more strategic, and profitable relationships with their customers, suppliers, employees, and community stakeholders.

Her clients include resource companies, utilities, regional and provincial governments, and financial institutions. Most recently, she worked with a financial institution to design and implement a highly successful relationship-building program with eight stakeholder communities.

Ann is currently writing a new book dealing with stakeholder auditing and the development of nonfinancial measures of corporate performance. Her articles about this emerging field have been published in leading business media, and she has developed a reputation as a dynamic speaker on this and other topics.

Ann is a senior partner with CoreRelation Consulting in Vancouver, British Columbia, and is on the board of directors of Canadian Business for Social Responsibility. She lives in Burnaby with her husband and two teenage sons.

Index

202 • THE STAKEHOLDER STRATEGY

ethical accounting, 155, 156, 157,
160
ethical investing, 26–27
ethical screening, 152
ethics
basic principles, 83
in corporate culture, 81–83
cross-cultural differences, 12–14
and profitability, 17, 18–19, 22, 81
See also social responsibility
EthicScan, 11, 23
ethics codes, 81–82
ethnic communities, building relationships with, 53–61
evaluation. *See* social accounting;
stakeholder audits
experimentation, 80, 97

facilities design, to support collaboration, 90
Fair TradeMark Canada, 25–26
fair-trade organizations, 25–26, 144
Fifth Discipline, The (Senge), 98
financial capital, 46, 61
financial resources, and collaboration,
134
First Nations groups, 6, 131–132
First Tennessee Bank, 35
Flood, A. L., 22
focus groups
at Nortel, 73
in stakeholder audits, 178–179,
180
at VanCity Credit Union, 55–56,
60
Follett, Mary Parker, 62, 63–64, 79,
145
FOSTERing stakeholder collaboration, 62, 66–70
France, employee relations in, 13
Freeman, R. E., 47
frequent flyer programs, 24
Fukuyama, Francis, 13
Future Search, 103–104, 105

gainsharing. *See* profit sharing
gap analysis, 100–101, 117–118, 167,
174, 176–177
GATT (Global Agreement on
Tariffs and Trade), 9
gender differences, and collaboration,
134–135
General Motors Corp., 130
Germany
codetermination laws, 10
employee relations in, 13
Glaxo Wellcome, 76–78
Global Agreement on Tariffs and
Trade (GATT), 9
globalization
cross-cultural differences in values, 12–14
impact of, 8–9, 10–11
goals for stakeholder groups,
123–124, 167, 173
government relations, 113
Graves, Samuel, 18
Gray, B., 129
Green Bank, 41
green consumer movement, 22–23
Greenpeace, 22–23
"greenwashing," 12
groupware, 92–93
*Guidelines for Corporate Social
Performance,* 175–176

Harman, Willis, 39
Hart, Stuart, 36
Haskins, M., 150
Hawken, Paul, 38
Henderson, John, 90
Heskett, James, 18
Hewlett-Packard, 18
high integration relationships, 65
high-involvement organizations,
87–88
Hock, Dee, 85
Hosmer, LaRue, 18–19, 142
Housing Development Corporation
(HDC), 94–96

Berrett-Koehler Publishers

ERRETT-KOEHLER is an independent publisher of books, periodicals, and other publications at the leading edge of new thinking and innovative practice on work, business, management, leadership, stewardship, career development, human resources, entrepreneurship, and global sustainability.

Since the company's founding in 1992, we have been committed to supporting the movement toward a more enlightened world of work by publishing books, periodicals, and other publications that help us to integrate our values with our work and work lives, and to create more humane and effective organizations.

We have chosen to focus on the areas of work, business, and organizations, because these are central elements in many people's lives today. Furthermore, the work world is going through tumultuous changes, from the decline of job security to the rise of new structures for organizing people and work. We believe that change is needed at all levels—individual, organizational, community, and global—and our publications address each of these levels.

We seek to create new lenses for understanding organizations, to legitimize topics that people care deeply about but that current business orthodoxy censors or considers secondary to bottom-line concerns, and to uncover new meaning, means, and ends for our work and work lives.

See next page for other books from Berrett-Koehler Publishers

Other leading-edge business books
from Berrett-Koehler Publishers

Customers As Partners
Building Relationships That Last
Chip R. Bell

WRITTEN WITH PASSION and humor, this groundbreaking work provides step-by-step guidelines for enhancing long-term customer loyalty and achieving lasting success. Chip Bell offers insights on how to keep the quality of customer relationships central in every interaction by creating sustaining personal bonds—the true source of a company's profitability.

Paperback, 256 pages, 1/96 • ISBN 1-881052-78-8 CIP
Item no. 52788-256 $15.95

Hardcover 9/94 • ISBN 1-881052-54-0 CIP • **Item no. 52540-256 $24.95**

Getting to Resolution
Turning Conflict Into Collaboration
Stewart Levine

STEWART LEVINE gives readers an exciting new set of tools for resolving personal and business conflicts. Marriages run amuck, neighbors at odds with one another, business deals gone sour, and the pain and anger caused by corporate downsizing and layoffs are just a few of the conflicts he addresses.

Hardcover, 200 pages, 3/98 • ISBN 1-57675-005-1 CIP
Item no. 50051-256 $19.95

Corporate Social Investing
New Strategies for Giving (and Getting) Corporate Contributions
Curt Weeden
Forewords by Paul Newman and Peter Lynch

AUTHOR CURT WEEDEN unveils a 10-step "corporate social investing" plan which not only promises to improve a company's bottom line but should lead to an increase of $3 billion or more a year in business support for schools, healthcare institutions, civic groups, and other nonprofit organizations.

Hardcover, 250 pages, 8/98 • ISBN 1-57675-045-0 CIP
Item no. 50450-256 $29.95

Available at your favorite bookstore, or call (800) 929-2929

Put the leading-edge business practices you read about to use in your work and in your organization

D O EVER YOU WISH there was a forum in your organization for discussing the newest trends and ideas in the business world? Do you wish you could explore the leading-edge business practices you read about with others in your company? Do you wish you could set aside a few hours every month to connect with like-minded coworkers or to get to know others in your business community?

If you answered yes to any of these questions, then the answer is simple: Start a business book reading group in your organization or business community. For step-by-step advice on how to do just that, visit the Berrett-Koehler website at <www.bkpub.com> and click on "Reading Groups." There you'll find specific guidelines to help in all aspects of creating a successful reading group—from locating interested participants to selecting books and facilitating discussions.

These guidelines were created as part of the Business Literacy 2000 program launched by the Consortium for Business Literacy—a group of 19 business book publishers whose primary goal has been to promote the formation of business reading groups within corporations and business communities. Business Literacy 2000 is dedicated to providing you with tools to help you build a dialog with colleagues, share ideas, build lasting relationships, and bring new ideas and knowledge to bear in your work and organizations.

For more information on the Business Literacy 2000 program, guidelines for starting a business book reading group, or to browse or download the study guides that are available for our books, please visit our website at:

<www.bkpub.com>.

If you do not have Internet access, you may request information by contacting us at:

Berrett-Koehler Publishers
450 Sansome Street, Suite 1200
San Francisco, CA 94111
Fax: (415) 362-2512
Email: bkpub@bkpub.com

Please be sure to include your name, address, phone number, and the information you would like to receive.